H4G 547 821 2

D0504405

Jamie
King of the Kitchen

Jamie

King of the Kitchen

THE BIOGRAPHY OF THE MAN WHO REVOLUTIONISED THE WAY BRITAIN EATS

STAFFORD HILDRED AND **TIM EWBANK**

JOHN BLAKE

Published by John Blake Publishing Ltd,
3 Bramber Court, 2 Bramber Road,
London W14 9PB, England

www.johnblakepublishing.co.uk

www.facebook.com/Johnblakepub   facebook

twitter.com/johnblakepub   twitter

Previously published as *Arise Sir Jamie Oliver* in 2009
This edition published in hardback in 2012

ISBN: 978 1 84358 503 9

All rights reserved. No part of this publication may be reproduced, stored in a
retrieval system, or in any form or by any means, without the prior permission
in writing of the publisher, nor be otherwise circulated in any form of binding
or cover other than that in which it is published and without a similar
condition including this condition being imposed on the subsequent publisher.

British Library Cataloguing-in-Publication Data:

A catalogue record for this book is available from the British Library.

Design by www.envydesign.co.uk

Printed and bound in the Great Britain by CPI Group (UK) Ltd

1 3 5 7 9 10 8 6 4 2

© Text copyright Stafford Hildred and Tim Ewbank 2012

Papers used by John Blake Publishing are natural, recyclable products
made from wood grown in sustainable forests. The manufacturing processes
conform to the environmental regulations of the country of origin.

Every attempt has been made to contact the relevant copyright-holders,
but some were unobtainable. We would be grateful if the
appropriate people could contact us.

Contents

Chapter One

Early Starter

The Cricketers, an inviting hostelry in the picturesque village of Clavering, in the heart of rural Essex, is everything an English pub should be. The elegant timber-framed building dates right back to the sixteenth century and inside the atmosphere is warm and welcoming and generally full of highly satisfied customers. This fine freehouse sells a range of good British beers. There is a remarkable wine cellar and the kitchens serve high-quality meals every day of the year. Not surprisingly, licensees Trevor and Sally Oliver are delighted by the recommendations their hospitality and food have produced from the English Tourist

1

Board, Egon Ronay, Michelin, the AA and just about everyone who has ever been fortunate enough to have eaten there. But they also have another production who is doing them rather proud as well, their fast-talking son Jamie.

Today he is internationally famous as the Naked Chef, the television phenomenon who has turned on millions of viewers from Sidcup to Sydney with his delicious high-speed food and high-energy friends in the most refreshing cookery series in decades. But some diners with long memories recall the day when a globally unknown ten-year-old Jamie managed to empty The Cricketers of staff and customers in about five seconds flat.

Bored in the long school summer holidays, he thought it would be a fun idea to let off some stink bombs in the bar. He decided it was sure to amuse his friends from the village who cheerfully sniggered in the background and egged Jamie on. He did not stop for long to consider the consequences, because Jamie Oliver has always been game for a laugh. Never one to shrink from a challenge, the mischievous youngster could not resist completing the dirty deed. Then he and his young pals scarpered as quickly as they could run.

To say that hard-working landlord Trevor Oliver did not see the joke is something of an understatement. Reliable observers of the scene recall that steam was distinctly visible coming from both ears at high speed. Trevor was absolutely furious because the smell was so awful that his customers couldn't have left any quicker if the place had been on fire. From the moment the first nose twitched over the roast beef to the last diner rushing into the car park took only two or three minutes. It was that bad. Jamie and his pals were watching the scene from behind a fence almost helpless with laughter.

The village chums thought it was the funniest stunt in ages and rushed home to tell their brothers and sisters. Jamie was left with his hilarity swiftly turning to horror as he saw people spluttering and getting into their cars and driving off. Jamie had tears running down his face as he watched the results of his prank unfold before his very eyes. But gradually, even at that early age, the full consequences of his actions were not beyond him. He knew that emptying the pub in record time was bad news for business.

Jamie remembers the result very clearly. He says, 'Thirty people left without paying and my old man gave me the hiding of my life. If there is one thing in my life I should apologise for it's that. It was absolutely unforgivable.'

Trevor was furious that his son should be so ridiculously reckless with the family business. He had no hesitation in handing out a suitable punishment to his high-spirited son. But he found it hard to do it without looking Jamie in the eye because he knew that then he would probably burst out laughing.

Trevor Oliver is in possession of precisely the same sort of irrepressible sense of humour as his son. And had the stink bomb attack been mounted on some other establishment, he would most certainly have seen and shared in the joke. But in his own pub, during a busy lunchtime, he could not believe that Jamie could have been so stupid. And it took him some time even to begin to appreciate the funny side.

But it was also extremely untypical. Certainly he might always have been the boy with the wickedly unrestrained sense of humour. But Jamie Oliver is remembered by everyone who knew him growing up as a lad in Clavering as a sunny, good-natured youngster who was full of fun and highly unlikely to commit malicious acts of commercial disaster to his hard-working father.

'It was a fabulous place to grow up,' says Jamie, not caring in the slightest how corny this might sound. 'And I had a wonderful childhood with a wonderful family.'

Villagers were a shade resentful at first of the newcomers who came to take over their local, with little regard for the joys of a late-night lock-in until the early hours. Trevor Oliver was determined to do much more than smile at the few aged regulars who loved to languish over their pints. But he cleaned the old place up from top to bottom and smartened up its appearance, as well as making a whole host of structural improvements.

Yet Trevor and Sally were always very well aware of the impact of all their alterations. They knew they needed to attract new customers who would come to enjoy the growing menu but they still had plenty of time for the locals who regarded The Cricketers as part of the social scene. To this day, they make sure that customers are just as welcome to come and enjoy a leisurely pint or two as those who order a full meal.

The Cricketers remains an integral part of Clavering. It is a quiet, rambling village, happy to be by-passed by busy nearby through-roads like the M11. It is still a place where everyone knows his neighbour and naturally watches out for them. Cars and houses are still often left unlocked. It was certainly an idyllic place to grow up. Even as a child, Jamie was a relentlessly social animal and he was always at the centre of a lively gang of rascals.

His earliest memories are of the days when he and his gang used to wander freely around the beautiful countryside. Their time was mainly much more usefully employed scrumping apples or making dens and playing cowboys and indians in the woods. Local farmers knew the lads and turned a blind eye to their activities around the area. Geographically, the village of Clavering might be in Essex but its peaceful unspoilt acres seem a world away from the more familiar image of the urban Essex of Billericay or Basildon.

'They were never any trouble, those lads,' said a village elder who asked to be identified simply as Dan. 'Young Jamie was a very nice lad. When my wife was ill and I was out at work, he knocked on the door one day and asked if she needed anything from the shops. No one told him to do it. He was only 11 or 12 but he knew she was stuck inside all day and he wanted to help. He fetched her some groceries and she reckoned she spent the rest of the day talking to him. My wife was a very good cook and they used to spend hours talking about recipes and meals. She knew some very old country recipes that came down from her mother. They're not in any cookery books, they were just in her head and Jamie was fascinated by that. He always wanted to know how well a certain meal had gone down at a big occasion and she loved telling him. We never knew another boy who was interested.

'My wife came from a big farming family in Norfolk and she used to tell Jamie about the great meals they prepared for big occasions like Christmas and when the shoot was on their land. He loved hearing her talk about having to pluck 20 pheasants at the crack of dawn so she could get everything ready for all the "guns" and the "bush-beaters" at night. He was dead inquisitive, was young Jamie, and when I got home she reckoned she was worn out with answering his questions. But he used to come quite a lot after that and he was always full of life and laughter.'

Jamie's parents originally come from Southend where he was born on 27 May 1975, which was also his father's twenty-first birthday. He mischievously told one interviewer that he was actually conceived on the end of Southend Pier.

'I said it for a joke and it ended up in print,' said Jamie. 'When it appeared, I had this telephone call from my mum saying, "Everyone will think I'm a slapper." But I could hear my dad laughing in the background.'

His mum was born Sally Palmer and she used to work in a bank before she met his father and they joined forces in running pubs and restaurants as well as in marriage. The couple are still as devoted today as they were in their courting days.

Sally was first taken by the twinkle in Trevor's eye and the ease of his warm sense of humour. Trevor was one of many men who took notice of Sally's blonde good looks and attractive figure. But it was his ability to make her laugh that was the first main attraction.

The Olivers are well known among their friends for having the happiest marriage around. Trevor was delighted when he realised soon after they met that she shared his enthusiasm for building up a good business together. 'Not everyone wants to work with their husband or wife all day every day,' says Trevor. 'Some people enjoy time apart but to Sally and me it has been like a bonus working together.'

Childhood friends are not at all surprised that the marriage has thrived. Trevor always wanted to build up a business and he often talked of one day running his own pub or restaurant. 'He has always had this amazing drive and confidence in his own ability,' says one friend from Southend. 'He believes that anyone can achieve anything if they try hard enough at it. He has no time for whingers and shirkers and people who blame others for their lack of success. I knew he would make something of himself and, when he met and married Sally, I was even more sure. She is like a female version of him. She is very pretty and feminine but underneath she is a really strong, focused woman. And they have hardly changed since they were youngsters.'

Trevor and Sally Oliver's famously long and happy relationship has influenced Jamie deeply. Even as a boy he noticed that his parents seemed to enjoy life and laugh a lot. 'They were always really busy, but they always had time for each other and to have a laugh,' says Jamie. 'I suppose you couldn't work that closely together without getting on well but it was more than that. My sister Anna-Marie and I were included in the laughter, and in the pub it always seemed like no one from outside could ever do anything to hurt our little world.'

The Cricketers was completely renovated from top to bottom by the Olivers. They bought the sleepy, shabby old pub when Jamie was still a baby. They knew it would be a long-term project but they could see the potential of the drab and frequently empty village pub in a time when a full range of pub food meant a selection of different-flavoured crisps in many establishments. And, to a huge extent, Jamie has learned from his father's example.

Jamie's father is very much his hero and the inspiration for at least some of his boundless self-confidence. 'Dad taught me to believe that anything is possible,' says Jamie simply.

'My old man is a mega hero. He is quite definitely my living example of how to act and how to behave. If he says he will do something then "Boom". It's done. I am not as good as that, but I am learning all the time and maybe I am half as good as that.

'My dad was the true gastro-pub inventor 25 years ago. The Cricketers has been chocker for more than half that time but when he arrived in Clavering the pub was disgusting. It was just a drinkers' pub with the locals calling in for their pension's worth of Guinness.'

Jamie's earliest memories are of watching how hard his parents worked. He noted that some of his young friends had parents who arrived home at five o'clock and slumped in front of the television. Others did not stir from their armchairs all day. With typical indiscretion, Jamie would return home with all sorts of stories of all sorts of more indolent lifestyles. But his father would simply explain his firmly held view that if you want to get anything out of your life, then you have to put something in. Trevor Oliver did not criticise the work-shy of Clavering. The eternal tact of the natural 'mine host' taught him not to let the conversation veer towards the controversial. Instead, he preferred to get his message across by example.

The Cricketers certainly gave him plenty of scope for hard work as it was sadly run down when the family arrived. But Trevor and Sally Oliver could see the potential and they had a dream to restore the historic inn to something of its old splendour. And they knew they would never be able to do that on the few rounds of drinks the customers bought. They knew that the future was food and not the third-rate 'soup in a basket' style of fare that still predominated in the mid-70s in English pubs. The Olivers wanted to serve the finest meals for miles around.

Jamie grew up watching his parents' dream come gradually and steadily true. 'Dad put a menu together, and put a buffet out,' says Jamie. 'People would just walk in and walk past at first. But then one person would stop, then two, three, four started to pick up. When I was about six years old, there was a massive turning point. He got a top chef in from Southend and paid him more than he was paying himself and my mum until he got the pub's reputation up to scratch. He started with 30 covers, moved on to 40 covers and it soon went up and up. After 20 years, he was serving the best pub food in Essex. When I look back, I am pretty proud and impressed by his timing. To me, Dad is the true guru of pub food.'

Trevor Oliver never believed in gimmicks or expensive advertising. He couldn't afford it and he wanted to build up his business so it became its own best advertisement. Trevor loved to see a customer with a smile on his face. He knew he was a walking advert who would bring in new business. He believed that simple word of mouth could make or break any catering enterprise and he made an enormous effort to deliver good-value, good-quality food at all times. Any rare complaints were dealt with head on. Even when they were being particularly difficult, Trevor knew that the customer was always right. If anyone was not satisfied, they would be dealt with fairly and courteously and often won over with a dish that was more to their taste.

'We never wanted anyone to leave The Cricketers unhappy,' says Trevor. 'I suppose it sounds obvious, but so many businesses seem to regard the customers as a bit of a nuisance. To me, they were the whole point of the exercise. They still are.'

It was like living a lesson in setting up and running your own restaurant and it was the one lesson that attracted young Jamie's full attention.

He reflected later how lucky he was to have such an upbringing. He witnessed first hand the ups and downs of running your own business. And Jamie always loved the social side of the job.

'Most people are interesting and worth talking to if you approach them the right way,' he says. 'My dad was just brilliant at making people feel welcome. He made them feel as if they were valued guests in our home, which in a way I suppose they were. And it's no surprise that many people who arrived as customers have turned into lifelong friends.'

As he grew up, Jamie gradually realised that one of his father's great skills was to maintain the same cheery public front out in thc pub, even if there was a crisis in the kitchen thanks to a sudden power cut or a chef not turning up for work on time.

Trevor and Sally were well aware that their improvements and changes to the village pub might not get the approval of everyone in Clavering, so they went out of their way to take on board as many of the views of the villagers as possible. There were a few old-fashioned drinkers who were fond of the original pub as a homely hovel, ideal for a quiet pint, but they were steadily won over by the tasteful nature of the alterations and the unfailingly warm welcome they received. And the pub gradually became a key employer in the village as many local youngsters did their first shifts of paid employment under the watchful eye of Trevor Oliver.

In those days, deep in the country and far from any major towns or cities, it was hard to get good fish. It was only delivered on a Tuesday and a Thursday and at The Cricketers they made a big feature of this. Jamie says, 'I remember my dad shaking his head one day because a woman had complained about the fish. It was as fresh as you like. Even I knew that and I was eight years old. Dad said, "Son, we have to educate some of these people. They are just too used to the frozen stuff." '

Nowadays, that education seems to be more or less complete and The Cricketers sells fresh fish every day of the week and their customers love it.

The skilled chefs employed at The Cricketers always made their own pasta and even though the theme in the kitchens was traditional English food, everything was done properly under Trevor's stern control. The steak and kidney pie was made with the help of a half-decent bottle of red wine. The Cricketers has been extremely popular for years now. It took a long time and many hours of careful budgeting to build the business and, at the beginning, money was often very tight.

But Jamie and his sister never wanted for anything

and, as the business grew more prosperous, they were always taught to be discreet about the family finances. Some of Jamie's young friends' families were very hard up and, even as a youngster, Jamie knew how to be thoughtfully tactful. His father taught him that the really successful restaurant is not about money but about providing an excellent meal and an enjoyable experience to its customers.

Jamie's mother Sally runs the business side and she is also a very good cook. Sally had a huge influence on Jamie during his formative years and some of his earliest food memories are of her mouth-watering desserts. Sally taught her son to use local ingredients wherever possible and she spent hours with him in the garden or in local hedgerows picking fruit. Years later, Jamie said, 'I know it's not rocket science, but blackberries from the bush are never like shop-bought ones in punnets. They always taste so much fresher.'

Jamie loved going with his mum to collect strawberries and raspberries for fruit to make jams and summer puddings and he regularly made himself sick by stuffing more of the succulent fruit into his mouth than their basket.

There is a great catering tradition in the Oliver family and all the relations enjoy nothing more than meeting up over delicious family meals. Two of

Jamie's uncles are cooks, as well as his parents, and all members of the family have a great interest in eating out. They were a very close family and food was at their heart. Jamie loves that traditional Sunday roast family feeling of closeness that was such an integral part of his growing up and tries to incorporate it in his recipes. Nowadays, he says, 'I'm not changing the world but you have nice times round the table, you know.' The importance of a family eating together and sharing their thoughts of the day over a well-prepared and leisurely-eaten meal is something which Jamie enjoys and believes in.

Not surprisingly, the catering business interested Jamie from as far back as he can remember. He loved the cheery hustle and bustle of the kitchens and constant throughput of fresh produce being swiftly prepared into tasty-looking meals.

Cooking was something that has been in his blood from a very early age and that caused plenty of disasters. He recalls cheerily, 'As a kid, I would put things in Mum's Aga and I would leave them in to cook overnight. When I came back in the morning, they would be like volcanic dust, like you had just cremated your grandmother.'

Sadly for the sake of posterity, Jamie cannot recall in detail the historic first meal that he cooked, though at the same time he can't remember a time when he was not keen on catering. 'I was very, very young when I started taking an interest in the kitchen,' he says. 'I started cooking regularly when I was about eight as a weekend thing. But when I was really young, my mum taught me how to make an omelette and I found I was good at it. That was a lovely feeling of satisfaction of actually creating something out of something else. I was fascinated by making proper omelettes and for a couple of years that is all I did. Then later, I used to make small pizzas, awful bits of dough, terrible tomatoes and horrible cheese. I used to cook them for my friends when I was about seven or eight. I remember thinking they were excellent but they were horrible! Then I made trifle and it sort of went on from there, really.'

Boyhood friends recall that The Cricketers was an unofficial meeting place for the gang. There was always a glass of lemonade and something delicious to eat.

'We seemed to be starving most of the time,' said one early pal, 'so it was natural for us to congregate where we might get something to eat. Jamie's dad didn't like us getting in the way of the customers but if the pub was closed or quiet we used to get in and I don't think we ever came away without something to eat and drink. It just seemed like such a fun place to be. And the food was always fantastic. Jamie was always trying out new tastes on us. I remember when he brought us some courgettes he was absolutely bursting with enthusiasm for this weird new vegetable that tasted a bit strange to us lot. Only Jamie could get worked up about courgettes. But he also gave us prawns and chicken legs and all sorts of things that we never saw at home. We always seemed to be hungry, so Jamie was always very popular.'

From a very early age, Jamie was desperately keen to join in the camaraderie of the kitchen. To the wide-eyed young boy, the chefs looked like the most glamorous figures in the world. They rushed around shouting out orders and putting together fantastic spreads, usually while having highly animated and unrepeatably rude conversations at very high volume. Jamie did not quite follow the joke, but he joined in the laughter when his father tried memorably to persuade one chef to moderate the language as he asked him with a grin, 'Why do you have to cook at the top of your voice?'

As an angelic-looking little blond-haired lad, he also got a great deal of attention from the customers. He looked as if butter would not melt in his mouth, but Jamie's parents were already finding out that their energetic young son was a real handful.

Jamie was just seven years old when he almost drowned in the bath while fearlessly performing a daredevil stunt. 'My parents had just bought a large corner bath so I decided to try it out,' he recalls. 'I went flying along the landing into the bathroom and jumped straight in, but I knocked myself out cold. Mum was getting dressed in her bedroom and she had heard the noise and came to see what was going on. With only half her clothes on, she rushed me downstairs, past all the surprised customers in the restaurant and out to the car. Then she drove me 50 miles to hospital in Cambridge in a complete panic. The doctors said I was concussed yet otherwise none the worse for wear. But I could easily have drowned.'

Even this hair-raising emergency was not enough to persuade Jamie to curb his adventurous, all-action attitude to life. 'I was a bit wild and I think the first accident might have knocked some of the sense out of me because it happened again,' said Jamie. 'Soon after the bath accident, I thought I would try flying because I was the proud owner of a pair of Superman pyjamas. I went hurtling down the stairs and knocked myself out again. This time, however, Mum didn't waste time taking me to hospital but to the local GP. By the time we arrived at the surgery, I had come round and was sent home after a check-up.' Jamie says dryly now that he definitely would not want to look after a child like him.

'When I was younger, I used to dream I could fly. I can recall quite clearly that when I was about five I dreamt of hovering above the sofa. In my vivid imagination, I felt I could float wherever I wanted to go. That led me into all sorts of painful crash landings until I finally realised how hard the ground was!'

Jamie loved living in a busy pub full of people constantly coming and going, and he desperately wanted to join in and become a part of it. His dad and his workers seemed like the most enjoyable gang in the world and he simply could not wait to join it. And even more than that, he wanted to get some pocket money. Cash had a way of burning a hole in Jamie's pocket that has hardly changed with time. There was always a new toy car or comic that he wanted, so he always seemed to be short of money. Jamie's father had a very simple and old-fashioned attitude to handing out money. You first have to do some work to earn it. He did not believe in simply handing out cash, even to his children. He believed that handing out endless cash to kids was the wrong way to behave. It taught them nothing about the value of money and it was a certain way to spoil the child. Trevor Oliver is the epitome of a loving father, but he worked very hard to build a better life for his family and he wanted to show his children from their early days that there was a clear link in life between effort and reward.

'I wanted to have some pocket money to spend and Dad told me that I had to earn it,' said Jamie. 'I thought washing up was perhaps not macho enough for a cool and sophisticated eight-year-old. I decided that most of the hardcore action was in the kitchen with the real men and that is where I wanted to be.'

The principle of the paramount importance of hard work on the way to a happy and successful life was thus instilled in Jamie at a very early age. His father made sure both Jamie and his sister Anna-Marie worked for their pocket money because he was convinced it would teach them the value of things.

Jamie has been fascinated by food for as long as he can remember. When he was only eight years old he would find regular employment podding peas, peeling and chipping potatoes and pestering the chefs for more responsible jobs at The Cricketers. He was paid £7.50 for two afternoons' work and he was delighted. 'Think how many penny chews you can buy with that.'

Trevor Oliver recalls, 'Jamie wangled his way into the kitchen, and by the time he was 12 years old or so he was getting to be pretty useful.' Not that he praised him too highly at the time, for Trevor was always a hard taskmaster when it came to supervising his workers and Jamie was no exception, just because he happened to be his son. But Jamie worked hard and learned aspects of working in the kitchen. His proud father Trevor later noted, 'When he was still only 14, it was quite usual for him and another chef to cook 100 or 120 meals on a Sunday night.'

Jamie has different memories of his learning curve. He reckons that by the time he was 11 years old he could julienne vegetables like a professional, and when he was only 15, the head chef at the Star in nearby Great Dunmow was confident enough of his culinary abilities that he put him in charge of a section.

Jamie spent a great deal of his boyhood helping out in his father's pub. Living above the business is not always easy, but Jamie revelled in having his home right at the hub of the village. He loved it always being busy and people coming and going all the time. Jamie is not a solitary person and happily admits that he can quickly tire of his own company if left alone too long. His parents had moved in and took over the inn soon after Jamie was born, so his total childhood was spent in the most social surroundings.

Being brought up on licensed premises has helped to give him a natural ease with people from all walks of life and of all ages. 'It was quite an amazing experience growing up in a country pub with all these different characters coming in every day,' he said. 'There was always something going on and always something happening. We were always taught to smile and be polite to people and make them welcome. So many of my dad's ways were right, that I find myself following them even now. "People want to feel pleased to be here," he used to say and I suppose it sounds so obvious. But over the years I've seen loads of restaurants where people plainly did not feel pleased to be there. Dad loved his job and he reckoned it was because he was interested in people. "Sometimes it only takes a smile to brighten up a customer's day," my dad used to say and many's the time nowadays that I think how right he was.'

Jamie cannot bear rudeness and slackness in any catering establishment. He seethes when Britain is accused of being second-rate in this department and always speaks up passionately on the country's behalf.

Jamie loved working in a place where other

people were relaxing. His father taught him the importance of listening as well as talking and regulars in Clavering always found young Jamie to be a genial and attentive companion. 'I would be sitting there talking to old men who would give me a mini-glass of Guinness and I would feel really grown up.'

Jamie was taught early on that customers need to be made to feel comfortable as soon as they enter an eating establishment. 'If they've never been inside before, they might feel a little unsure or awkward and the sooner you can put them at their ease, the sooner they are going to sit down and start enjoying themselves,' says Jamie. 'It sounds blindingly obvious, I know. But you can walk into a lot of restaurants and be left standing there like a lemon and it sets completely the wrong tone for the evening. Eating out should be a special experience. My dad drilled into me that people came to The Cricketers to be entertained. Often they were celebrating a birthday or a promotion or an anniversary and if you make that celebration a bit more enjoyable, they are all the more likely to come back again and tell their friends.

'I suppose I'm lucky because I do genuinely like people, which I have found is a huge help in life,' says Jamie. 'Most people have a nice side or something interesting to tell you, if only you take the trouble to find out what it is. And food is such a great leveller. Everyone likes to eat good food, so if you can serve that up to people you are half-way there.'

Customers remember Jamie as an attentive presence around the pub. Bryan Stephenson, a regular who used to drive over from a neighbouring village for supper a couple of times a week, said, 'Even as a young boy, he was very polite and helpful to the customers. He would come up and ask what we thought of our meal or if we wanted some more pepper or another drink, as if he was really interested in whether or not we were enjoying the meal. He would have a laugh as well but even as a young boy in his early teens he was just like his dad. He had that keenness to please and attention to detail. Lots of people are surprised he has become so famous but I always thought he would do well. He stood out even as a youngster. Good luck to him, I say.'

And Neil Weekes, who played football for Clavering as a young man, remembers Jamie 'always with a smile on his face. We would go to the pub after the game and Jamie would be helping to serve us our scampi and chips even though he was only about 11 or 12. He was a really nice, friendly lad. The pub had a great family atmosphere. But then, it had a great family running it.'

Jamie's parents worked very long hours to build up the business but they always tried to cover for each other so one of them was available for the children. Even though they lived above a busy pub, Trevor and Sally were always careful to preserve some privacy and they made sure there was always some special family time scheduled into every day. And they recognised the benefit of having regular family breaks.

'Being a publican is incredibly hard work,' says Jamie. 'You can be on call 24 hours a day and it is hard to ever properly relax. So Dad always made sure that he made the time for us to have proper family holidays. He took us away every single year to the Canary Islands, Cyprus or Madeira just to relax and get spoilt.

'But the place we always went back to every year was the Norfolk Broads. We used to hire a motor cruiser and go all over the place. Norfolk was fantastic. We would wake up early and there would be mist across the water and it was incredibly peaceful. We would take Nan and Grandad or an uncle or two. It was always good fun. And the boats were cool with pull-out beds, pull-out telly, pull-out oven, pull-out seats, pull-out everything. I found it fascinating. In the mornings Mum would do really good fry-ups for breakfast. Then we would pull back the big roof. It was always a convertible. And I would sit on Dad's lap and help drive the boat. We would stop at little beaten-up old sheds for free-range eggs "fresh this morning". The farm would be a mile up the track and they would trust you to put your money in the little pot and everyone always did. Then we'd explore little villages along the way and anchor in a broad, which was like a huge lake, for lunch. We would muck about in the dinghy and swim off the side of the boat and fish for little perch, roach and eels. At the end of each day, we would drop anchor and set up a barbecue in fields by the river. It was great.'

The freedom of the great outdoors has long appealed to Jamie. He loves to have plenty of space and as a boy he would walk for miles around Clavering, building dens, exploring woods and damning up streams. The gang would meet at Jamie's house to pick up as many supplies as they could snaffle and then set off into the country. Sometimes there would just be two or three, although on occasions there were as many as a dozen of them roaming the countryside. The local farmers knew them all by first names, kept a protective eye on them and gave them their freedom so long as they kept away from the machinery. The link between the people and the land is still strong in a place like Clavering and to this day Jamie is determined to return when he finally tires of the city.

Jamie was generally the leader of the group. He was not exactly bossy but he had a strong personality and a ready wit and he had a natural knack for making the others follow his ideas.

But as he grew older he became more and more involved in The Cricketers. His father came to rely heavily on his cooking skill and his capacity for long hours of hard work. Jamie is very keen to shrug off some of the suggestions that he was some sort of amazing child prodigy in the kitchen. The truth is that he saw cooking at first as just a way of earning some money and helping his dad out at the same time. He liked the work certainly, but insists, 'I didn't really become passionate about it until I was about 14 or 15. And I always came second in competitions.'

He never liked that, he admits, as he possesses a fiercely competitive spirit underneath that genial exterior. Jamie smiles, 'I believe you always have to try to be the best at whatever you do, even if it is scrubbing potatoes.'

Trevor and Sally Oliver were very caring parents

but they could be firm, too. And Jamie's enthusiasm for having long hair was a constant cause of friction. He couldn't understand why anyone should be allowed to control something so personal as his hair length and they couldn't understand why he wouldn't smarten himself up like the other kids.

The bitter conflicts are still clear in Jamie's memory, 'My very worst haircut was when I was eight. I had a really cool Ian Brown sort of thing. But then my dad brought two little bruisers in from the tug-of-war team who both had crew-cuts with tramlines and said, "Don't they look smart?" Two days later, Dad took me to the hairdresser's, and I had a grade one all over. He's bald now, though, so I got the last laugh in the end.'

In many ways it was an idyllic childhood, and his early memories are full of tree houses, dens and hilarious fights with soda syphons when the pub was mercifully free of customers. One friend from those days recalls Jamie's unquenchable enthusiasm for practical jokes. 'He just loved to throw buckets of water over people. He thought it was the funniest thing in the world to soak another lad to the skin. Once, we hid round a corner, three of us with buckets ready to drench one of our mates. Just as he came round this wall we let fly. Only it wasn't our friend Dave as we expected, but the village postman. He was quite an old chap and it really took him by surprise. He was wet through and we were so surprised we forgot to scarper. We just stayed there mumbling apologies and in the end he even started to see the funny side. Fortunately, it was quite a warm day and he had almost finished his round so it wasn't as bad as it could have been. But Jamie was really upset. He likes a laugh but he hates to hurt anyone. Underneath that chirpy, easy-going exterior he is actually a very caring bloke. He was horrified that we had soaked the postie, but then he also knew that if his dad found out he would be in real trouble.'

Jamie loved jokes but he was always dead against doing anything that went too far. Some of the older kids in the village developed the sport of relentless door knocking, bringing residents out to their front doors to discover, of course, that their surprise visitor had already vanished. Jamie was happy enough to watch some of Clavering's more pompous occupants disturbed this way but he was quick to speak up when an elderly lady who was forced to walk with a frame was targeted. A friend recalls that Jamie was horrified that she was bothered. And when the older boys ran off, he presented himself at the door and asked her if she had any jobs she needed doing. He finished up posting a letter for her and she had her faith in human nature at least briefly restored. And Jamie successfully persuaded her would-be tormentors to leave the poor old dear out of their next round of hilarity.

Three of Jamie's closest friends as a boy were gypsy children, whose parents were brought to the area by the money to be earned potato picking. It was back-breaking casual work but the potato-pickers did not do it out of choice. Even the kids had to join in and Jamie was horrified when he realised how desperate for cash their families were. Jamie is still friendly with some of those gypsy kids today and neither he nor his parents judged them because they lived life on the move with no fixed address. And although they were sharp and streetwise, Jamie quickly realised his young friends did not even begin to share or comprehend his wide experience of food.

'They were nice kids but they had such a boring diet,' he said. 'They had never even seen decent food, let alone eaten it. The pub closed between three and six and we would be there in the back. I can still picture the scene now. I would be making baps of lettuce, ham and mustard, salami, smoked salmon and lemon and their eyes nearly burst out of their heads. We took it all to a clearing in the woods for a feast. These gypsies had never even tasted turkey and pickle before; they used to just about live on jam sandwiches. Imagine giving them smoked salmon! When I opened up the sarnie and squeezed the lemon on the smoked salmon they just went, "Wow!" That look on their faces was my first feeling of "this is really good" about food that I can remember. It was like showing a kid from 1800 what a VW Golf Convertible looks like.'

But the gypsy kids taught Jamie some things as well. When he went into their caravans, he found families even closer than his own. One particular pal had brothers and sisters of just about every age living happily together in restricted space. Jamie's abiding memory is of them all speaking at once and hugging and laughing with a warmth and openness of spirit that impressed even the son of an undeniably happy family. Everything was put on the table and shared, he recalls. Whether it was food or money or the spoils of some other unknown enterprise. Jamie once saw them dividing the slices of a loaf of bread equally so everyone had just two. That was all they had for tea but there were no complaints and the evening ended in a very voluble game of cards. Jamie says he has never seen a family with so little have so much in terms of love and affection from each other.

As he grew older, Jamie was keen to learn all elements of the catering trade. His father drilled it into him that running a successful pub or restaurant was not easy. Certainly it involved hard work and long hours but it meant keeping an eye on every aspect of the business. There is no point in serving wonderful meals if you're losing money on every plate, but if you do not deliver top-quality meals, then the only kind of reputation you're going to build up is a bad one. Trevor Oliver had his finger on the pulse of every different aspect of his business and he knew that one of the keys to success was buying. Jamie learned the vital importance of sourcing good ingredients first-hand from his hard-working father. He always bought good-quality seasonal fruit and vegetables.

There were a large number of Italian-run greenhouses and market gardens in that part of rural Essex and Trevor Oliver was tireless in tracking them down. He always attempted to get ahead of the game and tried to buy up the best produce before it was sent to market. Jamie gradually graduated to occasional delivery man and remembers, 'I used to talk to the tomato man on my CB radio. I was Beefburger and he was Ellio the Italian Stallion.'

Trevor built up a good relationship with his suppliers. He paid on time but he would not tolerate any sub-standard produce. The growers came to trust him and, as The Cricketers began to thrive, so the market for their fruit and veg was always there.

In those days, it was not considered remotely fashionable to wear a big white hat and make a lot of noise in the kitchen. And as a career option for style-conscious teenagers, it was certainly not to be taken seriously. Jamie found that he was regularly and mercilessly teased by some of his more conventional classmates for wanting to be a chef. Not that unkindly perhaps, but it was pretty obvious that in those days it was not exactly a cool career, or very macho. 'It was never a manly thing to do, be a chef,' recalls Jamie, who refused to have his ambitions even slightly diverted. He has never minded greatly what other people say about him. And nowadays he is, of course, wryly amused that he has the last laugh from what was once considered a joke career. 'But whether you are a carpenter or painter or a mechanic, you can make the job as exciting as you want. I love cooking. And so I have fun doing it. Now people seem to think it is rather cool.' The jokes were like water off a duck's back. 'Everyone got teased about something,' he says. 'I knew my real mates were not laughing at me so I just laughed along with it all.'

All-action Jamie had much more important things to do than worry what a few jealous classmates thought. He was far too busy having a good time. As he grew into his teenage years, fun-loving Jamie was always at the centre of any action. Teachers at Newport Free Grammar School certainly found him quite a handful. One schoolmaster, who prefers to remain anonymous, recalls a concerted campaign involving 'moving' pupils. 'Whenever I turned my back on the class to write on the board, I would hear the furniture start to move around. They seemed to think it was a huge joke to swap seats, and in some cases even desks, while my back was turned. So I would look back at the class and home in on one of the more helpful members of the class, and ask a question to move the lesson on, only to find it was Jamie Oliver, or someone even dimmer, staring balefully back at me. The first time it happened it was most disconcerting. And as young Jamie appeared to be at the centre of it, I appealed to the class one day not to waste precious time indulging in what I described as the "Jamie Oliver Shuffle". That provoked gales of giggles and the name stuck for a time, though I'm happy to say that from then on they seemed to think I had suffered enough.

'I have to say that academically it was clear early on that Jamie was never going to be a high flyer. He was not without ability but he loved larking around too much for anything of any substance to remain in his brain. As a boy, he had a face that betrayed just about every one of his impish emotions so you always knew if he was up to something. Board rubbers had an unnerving habit of dropping off the top of doors as you started a lesson when young Jamie was around. He would try to look innocent but his face gave him away. For all that, there was no malice in the lad and I heard more than one story reported back to the staffroom of Jamie and his pals stepping hard on any outbreak of bullying.

'There was one rather weedy young lad who came on the bus from a village not far from Clavering who was forever getting his sports gear pinched and ink flicked in his face. Today, that bullied youngster is a teacher himself and he told me that it became quite nasty and had him bunking off school to stay out of the clutches of the bullies. But when Jamie and his pals found out about it, they stood up for the lad and warned the older boys off. He didn't hit anyone, he just stood up to them and issued a few embarrassing remarks about the cowardice of people who pick on people who are smaller than themselves. That did the trick.

'I always thought Jamie was much brighter than his tests and exam results revealed. He had a gift for talking to people with the sort of honest, wide-eyed enthusiasm that is hard to resist. There is no side to him at all. I met him years after he had left school, just as he was starting to be seen on television, and he seemed to be the same sunny individual I remember shuffling round the classroom. Everyone needs some fun in their lives, even teachers. And Jamie could be relied upon to provide it.'

But Jamie's knack for getting into scrapes was legendary. Friends used to joke that if you threw a cricket ball up in the school playground it would land on Jamie's head. And the accident-prone side of his nature was never far away. Jamie had even knocked himself out on a third occasion as a child by crashing his tricycle into a wall. And, much later, he crashed a scrambling bike in a field near his home. 'My parents didn't know I was riding that bike as I was only 14 at the time,' he said. 'I passed out while I was on it. I think I was overcome by petrol fumes because earlier we had been adjusting the fuel mixture to increase the speed.'

Jamie was born bursting with energy and he has scarcely ever slowed down since. He loved to run across the fields near his home. His parents later moved from the pub to a luxury home three miles away. They wanted to get away from the relentless pressure of living over the shop and Jamie used the journey for regular exercise. 'I suppose I am lucky that I have always had a lot of energy,' says Jamie. 'Running around has never been any problem, I enjoy it. But sitting still is very difficult.'

Once his generous parents introduced Jamie to the concept of regular holidays to spice up a hard-working life he has loved the feeling of getting up, up and away from it all. He loves a quickly-arranged break somewhere new that he has never been before. But even on holiday he found he could manage to land himself in trouble. Jamie remembers, 'Holidays with my parents ended when I was 14, then school trips took over. I went on two skiing holidays with my class to France. I had already been skiing with my family when I was much younger so I wasn't a complete novice. We went to a place called Brand in Austria when I was six. At that age, I didn't seem to have any sense of danger or pain or disaster and my sister Anna and I were skiing in no time. But while Anna glided off elegantly across the mountain, as lovely people should, I just wanted to ski straight down from top to bottom as fast as I possibly could. Even really good skiers couldn't catch up with me. The following year, Mum said, "You're making me so worried, you go far too fast. I'll teach you how to do an emergency stop." And it was a good thing she did because the very next day I skied like a maniac through this red tape, which obviously meant "Danger", and I managed to do an emergency stop only a few feet from the edge of a cliff.'

That frighteningly fearless side to his nature used to give his poor parents plenty of anxious moments. They would try to reason carefully with him that he was shortening the span of his natural life expectancy many times over if he continued to refuse to take even a modicum of care. Jamie would nod wisely in agreement and assure them that they were absolutely right – and then continue to live life to its dangerous full at all times.

Jamie sees things slightly differently. 'By the time I went off with the school, Mum had bollocked me into shape enough to make me concentrate on what I was doing. We went out to France at Easter – 30 boys with a mission not only to ski, but to get hold of drink and fags and do whatever was forbidden, all of us fizzing with pure baby testosterone. It was a wonderful holiday.'

But one thing which Jamie did not instantly appreciate was the delights of European cooking. 'One thing I learned was that "Continental breakfast" actually meant stale bread and disgusting jam. And on that we were expected to ski for five hours, in theory one of the most demanding sports in the whole wide world,' he snorted.

As a teenager, Jamie preferred to start the day like most of his contemporaries with a traditional English breakfast – nice crisp fried bread to provide a platform for a couple of eggs and plenty of rashers of bacon alongside. This was definitely not on the menu in the budget accommodation used for the school trips, so Jamie decided to take direct and extremely popular action. 'So the following year I secretly took a little cooker with me – an old camping gas one – and a non-stick frying pan. We bought bacon and eggs at the local supermarket and did wonderful fry-ups for breakfast on our balcony.' He laughs loudly at the memory. The hotelier did not appreciate Jamie's firm rejection of his catering facilities, but he did not find out that the young man had set up his own kitchen on his balcony until it was late in the holiday and he decided to dismiss it as 'crazy English again' with a shrug of his shoulders.

Many of the crazes which dominate the waking

lives of schoolboys passed Jamie by. His hours were more often filled with hard work or scouring the countryside for adventure than playing with model railways or collecting stamps for an album. He laughs at the very idea. 'I used to collect beermats as a kid, which wasn't too much of a challenge for somebody growing up in a pub, but I pretty soon got fed up of that. I mean, what are you supposed to do with beermats when you've collected them? Apart from that though, I have never really had a hobby.'

All-action Jamie was never exactly deliberately rash as he hurtled through life, but at the same time he could never claim to be the most safety-conscious person in the kitchen as a young man. At 16, he damaged an artery in his hand in an accident that was very close to cutting short his career as a chef before it had properly begun. 'I picked up a tea towel that had been used to collect some broken china and a sliver of it severed my artery,' he remembers with a wince. 'Surgeons carried out micro-surgery to repair the artery and a damaged nerve and fortunately everything was OK.'

Typically, Jamie chooses to make light of the accident, but it was a terrifying experience for both him and his parents and it has left him with a lasting horror of his own blood and a passion for safety in the kitchen. Jamie is not the least bit squeamish about all the blood and guts he encounters at work, yet certain things can turn his stomach. 'I'm a bit weird,' he smiles. 'If I get a paper cut I faint but I can cut a pig in half and it doesn't bother me.'

And being accident-prone didn't just have repercussions for Jamie himself – others suffered on occasions, and did not always recover. He explains, 'When I was about 13, I had a fish tank with about 250 fish in it. It was beautiful, and when I woke up one morning all the fish had been completely cooked – the thermostat had gone on and all I had was 250 dead fish.'

Young Jamie's nose would most certainly never be found within the pages of a good book, or even a bad one. He says, 'Reading bores me to death as I am dyslexic. I have honestly never read a book from cover to cover in my life. And at school textbooks did my head in.'

But Jamie never allowed his dyslexia to become an excuse. He acknowledges that he does not really have the patience or the concentration to become a great reader.

In fact, Jamie admits to an affection for *The Secret Diary of Adrian Mole aged 13¾*, but insists now the book he has read most often is '*The Naked*

Chef, but only because I wrote it and had to check everything so many times'.

When he was younger, he struggled to sit still long enough to spend as long in front of the television as his classmates, but as a young child Jamie never missed *The Flumps*. Now he has grown up, his favourite *Star Wars* character is Chewbacca because 'he makes funny noises and is really hairy'. To this day, Jamie has a very active imagination and loves well-crafted cartoons and slapstick comedy.

Schoolfriends recall Jamie as a very peace-loving guy, but confirm that he is no softie. 'He was not so much a brave guy as completely fearless,' says David Stevens, a boy in the year below Jamie at school. 'I once saw him stand up to three much older boys who were punching one of the juniors in the toilets. It wasn't desperately vicious, but this young kid was having a hard time.

'He was a friend of mine and I was standing in the background kind of hoping not to get involved but not wanting to be so cowardly as to actually run away. Jamie came in and saw what was happening straight away. He just walked in front of my friend and looked the biggest guy in the face and said, "That's enough of that." And they stopped. There was something in the way he spoke, kind of quiet but confident, that gave the impression that underneath the smiley exterior he might be quite hard. I think the big guy knew him or something and he turned it into a joke and tried to make out it was one big laugh. Jamie laughed as well, but not with his eyes. Me and my mate scarpered but Jamie was our hero after that. He didn't have to do or say anything and I reckon most people would not have got involved.'

Jamie is convinced that somewhere deep inside him he has the ability to kill someone in extreme circumstances, if someone was attacking him or his family. It was years later when he admitted as much. He cannot remember his valiant schoolboy deeds in standing up to bullies but on a more general theme he is honest enough to admit that if he really had to he could use violence to protect himself and his family.

'I think everyone has the capacity to kill,' Jamie said frankly. 'I think that as you get older and you have a family and kids, you develop a sort of inner love that means you'd do anything to protect them. It would be easy to kill someone if they really threatened the ones you loved.'

Jamie started driving as soon as he could and he loved the freedom of movement that came with passing his test. In a sequence of flashy cars, he quickly became a familiar figure on the lanes and roads around Clavering. His flamboyant style behind the wheel soon earned him the attention of the local constabulary and, as a young driver in Essex, he was nabbed twice for speeding. Only he insists to this day that he wasn't speeding at all. He believes that the police just haven't got that much to do out there in the country, so they fill in their time slowing down anyone who looks like a potential speeder.

Jamie and his sister Anna-Marie have always been very close throughout their lives. But they are very different characters. Anna-Marie is famously together and down-to-earth, while Jamie admits he is far and away the more theatrical member of the family. He smiles as he admits, 'The first day I went to playschool I cried my eyes out and wanted my mummy. On her first day, she got straight in there and started organising people. Some things never change.'

Jamie's teachers were generally hard pressed to contain his irrepressible sense of mischief and not one of them predicted fame and fortune for the boy who could never ever be persuaded to sit still. Mrs Chris Murphy knew Jamie even before he arrived in her class at Newport Free Grammar School. She remembers, 'I first met Jamie when he was only three years old and we used to sit in the lovely gardens of his family pub in Clavering with our own children enjoying a relaxing drink in the sunshine.

'A few years later, I had him as a pupil and taught him on and off for five years after he started in my class in Year Seven. He was 11 years old by then. He was very lively and enthusiastic with an infectious laugh, very much as he is now. I'm a Geography teacher but I also did some reading. To be honest, I never thought he would go far, especially not as far as he has.

'I knew from The Cricketers where he grew up what a hard worker he was and of his interest in working in the kitchens. But we didn't do any cookery at school. And I am afraid the truth is that he did not excel at his lessons at all. He was much more interested in the band and in cooking. Jamie was music mad then and I always thought he might do well in that line. But it is very nice when former pupils succeed in whatever field of activity they choose to follow. It's lovely when you see former pupils do well. Jamie wasn't very good at spelling. He was in a group where we did puzzles and spelling games to try and improve his spelling. I look at his books and think his spelling is certainly all right now.

'Then it was an all-boys school. The school has gone mixed since then. And they have food technology now. It was an old traditional grammar school which went comprehensive towards the end of the Seventies. Jamie was a very nice boy and he was always very popular.'

Mrs Murphy is very proud of her old pupil and one of her most treasured possessions is a copy of his first book personally inscribed 'To Mrs Murphy, all my love, Jamie Oliver'. Mrs Murphy sought out her old pupil at a book-signing session in June 1999.

'Remember me?' I asked. "Of course I do," he laughed as he flung his arms round me. 'I've come for you to sign my book,' I said. "I still can't spell," he admitted.

'That doesn't seem to matter very much,' I replied. My street cred with my present pupils is high as I often use Jamie as a role model for what hard work can do for you in life. And I smile every time I see him on television, which is pretty often. What better motivation can there be for a teacher than a successful pupil, even one who can't spell?'

As a boy, Jamie used to go and watch his local football team, Cambridge United, but he was never a football fanatic. He loves the comradeship of being in a gang of mates going to a game, but he always used to make sure that they ate before they went because he reckoned the pies were seriously dodgy. Now he is based in London he follows

Arsenal, but he does not intend to let it rule his life. And these days, he rarely finds time to go. As he says, 'Since I have been a professional chef, I don't get much time to go to matches.'

Chapter Two

A Perfect Match

In his own words, Jamie was hopeless at school and he insists with a grin that whenever he put his hand up in English to make a contribution, the whole class used to chant mercilessly 'special needs'. It never bothered him in the slightest. 'I love a joke and I enjoy larking about,' he says, 'and if you dish it out you have got to be prepared to take it. My schooldays were a really happy time. I have to confess I took the mickey out of other people a lot of the time so I honestly did not mind the jibes. So long as there was at least a hint of humour about them. Perhaps if I had not been enjoying myself quite so much, I might have done better in class.'

But just before he was about to leave Newport Free Grammar School, his schooldays were considerably brightened by the arrival of one Juliette Norton. Jamie met 'Jools' at the school and his life was never quite the same again. He was just about to leave to go to college when she arrived to join the sixth form. He has never forgotten that first glimpse. At 16, she was already stunningly beautiful and Jamie always gives the same flip answer as to what first attracted him to Jools, 'She was very pretty and very clumsy in a sexy way. She had very long legs – and a great set of Bristol Cities.'

A schoolfriend recalls, 'He was totally dumbstruck when he first saw her. He often has his mouth open at the best of times, but that day you could have driven a bus in, a double-decker at that. He was totally transfixed by her and he stared at her so much I think she thought he was a bit slow. We could all see she was a cracker, of course. Any bloke who couldn't would need a guide dog, pronto. In the flesh, she has this sort of amazing quality of somehow glowing with a remarkable sexuality. Then she was so young it was mixed up with a wonderful coy innocence that definitely made her the pin-up of her year. But she didn't seem that interested in boys at all, really, and particularly not interested in Jamie. I think she liked him as a person because once he managed to pick his jaw up off the floor he resumed being the usual lively joker.'

There was competition for Jools's affections but she never seemed that interested in any of the early admirers who virtually queued up to ask her out. She smiled politely that she was busy, or washing her hair, or working and almost always the would-be suitors got the message.

For the first time in his life, Jamie's natural confidence let him down. He knew right from the first time he saw her that she was really special. He had had brief flirtations with girls before, but none of them had made his heart pound the way a glance from Jools did. She only had to catch his eye in the early days for him to blush crimson and be subjected to another round of mickey-taking.

They were friends for a long time before there was any hint of romance. Jamie was forced to worship from a distance but he gradually became more and more besotted. Friends recall that he would talk about her endlessly and always be trying to come up with new ways to make her laugh and notice him. He thought she was playing hard to get but Jools was simply in no hurry. Jamie was popular with other girls but that never worried her. Somewhere, deep down inside, she knew that they would be together, though it was Jamie's music and his ear-shattering stage presence on drums that first drove her to consider having him as something more than just another schoolfriend.

'She thought I was an idiot at first,' says Jamie. 'I know she did because she told me so herself. The first time she really liked me was when we did a big gig with the band. There were loads of people there and she liked the way I was drumming. After two years of just being friends, that was what finally did it. You can make of that what you will. To tell you the truth, I didn't ask any questions, I just thought, Thanks very much, Jools.'

But once they were together, they both knew it was serious. Jamie has a naturally sunny disposition, but once he was properly installed as Jools's boyfriend he felt his life was, in many ways, so much more complete. The young lovers were inseparable and friends use to tease them, 'Stop smiling at each other, you two, you're sickening.' Jamie used to pinch himself to make sure it was all really happening. He simply never looked at another girl once he was with Jools.

One of his happiest memories of their long and happy relationship is one of their first holidays together. It took some negotiating with both sets of parents to get away together, but Jools's mother and father were ultimately just as wise and understanding as Trevor and Sally Oliver. They could see before their eyes that something was happening to Jamie and Jools and they had enough trust and romance in their souls not to stop the young lovers going off together.

Jamie recalls fondly, 'When I was 17, I went to Crete with Jools. We saved up our money and rented an apartment overlooking the sea in a little village called Stalis. It is just a quiet family place with a few tavernas and a couple of bars, nothing mad. I was already working in restaurants then so I was knackered. The best part of that holiday was just falling asleep on the beach next to Jools in the beautiful late afternoon sunshine.'

Jamie was very anxious that their first trip away together should be a success. He wanted everything to be perfect with Jools and, in fact, at first he was guilty of trying too hard to ensure that they had the best meal, the best bit of beach to sunbathe on and the best bar to sit in and gaze into each other's eyes every evening. It was not until Jools gently calmed him down by assuring him that he only had to relax and be himself to make her happy that the holiday really took off. They talked and giggled into the night and discovered that they had so much in common in their attitudes about life and family and, one day, children, that everything seemed perfect.

Jamie started a catering course at Westminster College in 1992 at the age of 17. He felt it was his only viable option for the future. 'I had done so badly at school that there was no point in staying on,' he says frankly. 'Basically, I buggered about too much. The way my brain worked, I needed to see, touch and smell things. I enjoyed the practical side of learning and I did all right at Art and Geology because they were very touchy-feely subjects, but Maths and English were a nightmare.

'I came out of school at 16 with an A in Art and a C in Geology. It seemed like all I could be was an artistic geologist! Instead, I chose catering because it was the only thing I was any good at. In the pub I had grown up with professional chefs doing everything from scratch. I had been cooking since I was eight and, to be honest, I never really seriously considered doing anything else. I knew I didn't just want to stay at The Cricketers and work for my father, which was certainly one option. But that is his place and I think we both understood that there was only ever going to be one boss of that place while he was around and it certainly wasn't me.

Dad wanted me to get a proper training and earn good qualifications. He is a great one for being as professional as you can, whatever it is you happen to be doing.'

The arrival of Jools on the scene made Jamie grow up very quickly. All of a sudden he wanted to do more than simply hang out with his mates and drink too much. He still had a wide and lively circle of friends, of course, but with Jools he was instantly part of a couple.

Some of his friends were disappointed that wild man Jamie was slowing down, but he did not see it like that at all. 'I still clowned around after meeting Jools,' said Jamie. 'And I hope I always will. But often I do it with her. Jools has a great sense of humour and I really love making her laugh. I still have nights out with the boys and trips away with the boys but they are not the main thing any more.'

Some people said he was married long before the ceremony, that the partying stopped when Jools came on the scene, but that is not the case. It is the fun side of Jamie that Jools was first attracted to and she has a horror of ever turning into the sort of battleaxe-type wife who is forever waiting at the door with a rolling pin for her drunken husband.

'It's just not like that,' says a friend. 'It never was.

Our generation doesn't live like those stereotype figures of our parents' generation. Boys and girls have friends of both sexes they can have a laugh with and they have lovers that really do share all sides of their life.'

But Jamie still wanted to look after Jools and, to do that, he needed to kick-start a career of some sort. His love of food and experience in catering made it a pretty obvious choice. Westminster's catering department had a very good reputation which was why Jamie chose it, but as he was reluctant to leave home it meant a gruelling two-and-a-quarter-hour journey into college every day from deepest Essex.

It was not an easy life, but he did have help. Jamie used to get up at 5.30am in order to get to London soon after 8.00am and every morning his mother would make sure his day started with a full cooked breakfast. Even today, he insists that breakfast is his favourite meal of the day. And his mum Sally believed that her son deserved the best possible beginning to every morning. She rose early for the three years he was at college to prepare either the traditional full English breakfast or his other favourite, scrambled eggs, or an omelette made with left-over sausages, sliced up and fried and then folded inside the eggs.

Served with lashings of tomato ketchup, Jamie felt about six years old as he tore into the first comfort food of the day. Jamie says he always knew he had the best mum in the world, but those early-morning feasts before he took on a day in London proved it to him.

He had a head start on the catering front but everything else was a terrible shock to the country boy. 'College was so cosmopolitan. Coming from a village where there were only white people, on my first day at college I thought I was in New York,' he said. 'I had never really been to London before and I was really pent up about it. I had one of those leather pouches hidden under my shirt with my money in it. Every day I thought I was going to get mugged.'

Jamie was terrified when he spotted one student with dreadlocks, which were not normally sighted in the tranquil villages around Saffron Walden.

'Later, I found that quite cool,' said Jamie, 'but at the time I thought, Oh my God!'

He tried not to admit quite the extent of his shyness to Jools and his family when he got home but he did find those early weeks commuting to college very difficult. Gradually, he took to wandering around London a little and slowly his aversion to cities and his desperation to get back to his familiar safe and reliable countryside receded. 'I started to find London exciting instead of simply terrifying,' says Jamie. 'I loved the parks and the wonderful old buildings and, of course, I was entranced by the endless variety of famous restaurants. Not that I could afford to go in them, of course, but I loved looking at the impressive menus and dreaming that one day the all-powerful head chef would be me.'

At first, Jamie was less than delighted to discover that the course included a fairly large element of science at a higher level than the school syllabus, which had already had him struggling badly. 'It was a lot harder, but because I could now see the point of it and it clearly had relevance to what we were doing in the kitchen, it made sense to me,' he says. So instead of bunking off to the nearest pub and keeping out of the way, he buckled down and struggled with the subjects that had completely defeated him at school. Jools was proud of this new mature attitude and encouraged Jamie to work hard.

With his experience at the sharp end, Jamie's confidence grew as he discovered he could chop vegetables much faster than any of his lecturers. On his first day at college, his classmates watched his blade whirring with awe. And to their own later regret, they tried to copy his technique and rival his speed. By the end of the first week, his fellow students all had their fingers covered in blue plasters. So he earned a reputation as something of a cocky member of class. 'Oh, I *am* cocky,' smiles Jamie, 'but in the nicest possible way, I hope.'

Jamie surprised his closest friends and himself and worked very hard indeed, even though the concentration of the course on classic French cuisine did leave him deeply unimpressed.

'The public's requirements are definitely a lot simpler nowadays and more global,' he says. 'But I remember spending what seemed like months being taught how to make the perfect Béchamel sauce. I have never made it since and I have worked in Michelin star restaurants and even in France.'

Jamie scarcely clowned at all in class. He realised that this time the lessons really were worth listening to and he became an enthusiastic and model student. 'I realised that I was very privileged to be there,' he says. 'I knew one kid who couldn't afford to stay because his family went bust in the first term. He had to leave and I thought that was desperately unfair at the time. Mind you, I still do.'

After work, Jamie and his few friends on the course took an interest in exploring London and all its attractions. After one birthday party, they began a pub crawl that took in some of Soho's seedier night-spots and young Jamie found himself quite shocked at the sales techniques of some of the ladies of the night. They were so blatant and so young he was appalled at the danger they were facing as they earned their living.

But much of the time was spent working on the wide-ranging course and Jamie passed his exams with flying colours and gained his NVQs 1 and 2, national diploma and City and Guilds 1 and 2. He is very grateful for the grounding he received at Westminster and believes such courses are essential to provide the basic techniques and grammar of cookery in a wide range of styles and settings.

'It sounds a bit stuffy when you say it,' he observed later. 'But education can really open doors for you, and even someone like me, who basically messes up at school, can get his life together if he gets on the right course.'

Jamie's parents encouraged their son but they did not spoil him with large amounts of money to live on and he was forced to work to earn extra to help pay his way as he studied. He did all sorts of strange jobs. 'At college I used to earn extra money by washing cars,' says Jamie. 'I have never minded hard work so I put a board up offering to wash your car for three quid, which was loads of money then. And I got plenty of takers.

'Westminster is the best catering college in England and by the time I got there I was pretty good at all the technical stuff, and I finally settled down to the academic side. When I left, I got my diplomas and distinctions in my exams.'

Jamie did not quite know what had hit him when he arrived at the gates of the imposing Château Tilques. He was just 18 years old and the grand old building surrounded by sweeping lawns and carefully cultivated countryside had certainly been around for an awful lot longer than that. A helpful lecturer at Westminster College had pulled a few strings to land the would-be young chef some work experience at this elegant, up-market French hotel. Jamie was instantly awe-struck by the nineteenth-century splendour of the stylish hotel which was built on the site of a seventeenth-century manor house. Years later, in the run-up to the 1998 World Cup, Glenn Hoddle and the hopeful England players were not too relaxed either as they used the hotel to prepare themselves for their luckless campaign in the finals.

But, for young Jamie, it was very much more of a culture shock. Château Tilques is less than an hour's drive from the Channel port of Calais, but Jamie's nervousness grew with every unfamiliar mile. Today, the stylish conference hotel has a framed cover of Jamie's book in its reception area with the passage praising Château Tilques' role in his education as a chef carefully highlighted. But on Jamie's first visit, he was completely unknown and frequently very unhappy.

The elegant housekeeper Edith Boisseau, who still supervises breakfast at Chateâu Tilques, remembers young Jamie very well indeed. 'He looked so young and so lonely when he arrived and my English is not so good, but I knew he was missing his home and family from the start,' she said. 'Myself, I tried to make him welcome and to feel at home, but I know that in the kitchens they gave him a hard time. It is part of the training. And they teased him a lot at first. But, in the end, the chef told the others to leave him alone. The chef couldn't understand a word he said but he knew Jamie loved the work. He said that he treated food with respect, which was good.'

Jamie did not mind the long hours but some of the elaborate dishes he helped to prepare at Château Tilques shocked him. The hotel prides itself on top-quality, traditional French cooking and some of the sauces and many of the dishes took hours of intricate work to prepare. This was definitely The Fully-Clothed Chef. But Jamie did not dare to criticise. He was there to learn and he marvelled at the ancient skills the chef and his senior staff employed. And, in turn, when they saw the speed with which the young Englishman wielded his vegetable knife, they gave him a grudging nod of approval. Jamie worked extra hours because he found little to do in his time off.

But Elaine Fournier, from nearby Saint Omer, was a part-time waitress at the time and she liked the look of the shy young English boy. 'Jamie was so sweet,' she recalls. 'We were the same age and I have quite good English so I used to chat to him when we finished work. He was so missing his home and his family. He had photos of his family and his home, the pub in the country, and he showed them to me. He used to say he wished he was there. And I tried to make him feel welcome in France. I invited him to my home but he was so shy it never happened. He told me he had a beautiful girlfriend. Just when I was hoping he might take some interest in me, he started telling me all about this Juliette. He showed me her photo and my heart sank because she really was beautiful. In a way, it was better after that and we could just be friends. I did hope before that he would like me because he was very sexy, with long hair and strange clothes and always this smile. But after he made it clear about Juliette we relaxed and he told me of his other passion for a restaurant of his own. He told me how his father had built up this fantastic business with hard work over a long time and he wanted to do the same. He would say all that and then run to the telephone to talk again with Juliette or his family. He was a very nice boy and now I see him on television I tell my husband and my daughter that Jamie was my friend.'

The ghosts of the original aristocratic owners of Château Tilques are said to haunt the grounds. The hotel warns visitors: 'Our dear friends and guests, do not be surprised if late one evening, at the edge of the garden, in the tranquillity of the sleeping waters, you spy reflected in the moonlight the shadows of the knights who once upon a time occupied these premises.'

Jamie walked the grounds endlessly as he counted the days until his three-month spell in France was over. But he never saw any French noblemen. He was lonely and cut off and several times he considered heading for the ferry to go back to a land where people understood him. But he knew his father would feel he had failed, so he was determined to see his time out. Edith noted, 'He always knew how long it was before he went home. I would ask him how many days and he knew because he used to count them off one by one. But, by then, I think he liked us a little. The chef said he would work well, which is great praise from him. Now we all wish he would come back to see us again one day.'

Jamie was deeply relieved to be back in England and he had an emotional reunion with Jools. By then, they were very much a couple and they spent hours together dreaming about their future. She was going to make it as a top model and he was going to open this magnificent restaurant with diners fighting among themselves to get a table because the food was so wonderful. After he had formally left college, Jamie went to work in Antonio Carluccio's Neal Street restaurant because he was keen to learn from the legendary Gennaro Contaldo. The wise and experienced chef took enthusiastic young Jamie under his wing from the start and taught him his ways of making bread, sauces and fresh pasta.

Gennaro recalled fondly that Jamie would even come in at four in the morning to help him make the focaccio. 'He wasn't supposed to be there at that time but he wanted to learn so much,' said Gennaro, the Italian master of the kitchen. 'My God, he really was a help. And then I started to love him. What he made was so good, so colourful, so fresh. I used to eat it myself and the chef never eats his own food. I used to think, This is good. Bloody hell, he does it better than me.'

Jamie will always be grateful to Gennaro. He says, 'I worked my arse off to get his techniques. The recipe for his bread is in my book.'

Working with Gennaro had long been a strongly-held ambition of Jamie's. And he was not happy when anyone laughed at his ambitions. 'When I left Westminster, the lecturer said, "I want to see what everyone's ambition is and what you all want to do,"' recalls Jamie. 'Everyone else was saying that they wanted to go to work in exotic establishments like Le Manoir and the Ritz. I just put my hand up and said, "I want to learn how to make really good bread and pasta." Everyone took the piss out of me as though I was some boring little housewife. Now, looking back, I think it was quite an honest thing to say, really. I had an Italian friend who said, "If you want to make good bread, go and see Gennaro," so I did. And I went to work at the Neal Street restaurant as the pastry chef. I used to help him out by getting all his stuff out. I managed to start working with him in the middle of the night quite regularly. Gennaro is a fantastic guy and I loved watching him work. He has this brilliantly positive attitude to every single thing he does. He always wants it to taste perfect and he never tires of trying to improve things. I loved working with him and I learned so much about cooking. He was like my second father.'

Gennaro eventually moved on to work at Passione in London's Charlotte Street, which is very much Jamie's idea of an ideal restaurant. 'Italian food, really good value, really authentic, won't put you out of pocket.'

The *boulangers* in France had impressed the young Jamie with their speed and dexterity at making bread, but the experienced Gennaro taught Jamie to slow down his hands. He insisted that the real skill was as delicate and difficult to perform as making love to a beautiful woman. Jamie was quick to take the advice and adapted his bread-making accordingly.

Jamie actually began writing what was to become his first best-seller while he was working at Neal Street. He bought a typewriter and told Jools that he was going to write a cookbook. She laughed that he could not even spell, but he wasn't joking. Long before *The Naked Chef* was ever even dreamed of Jamie would tap away to record his thoughts on food and his favourite recipes. Putting them down on paper made them seem like real recipes and whenever he had settled on a particular new dish he was always keen to tell people about it.

'He always liked to communicate,' said a friend. 'Jamie is the most unsecretive person I know. He is so open. He always has been.'

Jamie never dreamed that his typed jottings would reach such an incredible worldwide audience, but when the offer came for a book to follow his TV series he had around one third of it written already in typewritten notes prepared five years earlier.

But writing the original notes that were to form the starting point of the book was very much a labour of love for Jamie. The enthusiasm that has made him such a popular television star is genuine and it comes from a natural passion for food and the positive role it can play in all our lives.

'A good meal can be a wonderful thing,' said Jamie. 'It can repair feuds, seal firm friendships and spark wonderful romances. I think the Italians are among the people who understand this most deeply. And the French, I suppose. Here in Britain, you can still be considered a bit of an oddball if you go on and on about cooking. And I should know. But I don't care if some people think I am strange. So long as I enthuse and interest others, that is fine.'

Chapter Three

family Sadness, and Joy by the River

Not every aspect of Jamie's young life was so eternally sunny. He was to experience the darker side as well. Jamie's much loved grandfather, Ted, died from a stroke when Jamie was only a boy and the memories are still painful to this day. Jamie was 11 when his grandfather had the stroke that tragically led to his death three years later at the age of 75, and he well recalls the heart-rending effects.

Jamie says, 'He was a handsome and fit man, but all that changed after his stroke. It took away his dignity and he found it hard to express what he wanted. I was quite shocked. It was not that he looked ill. He could still walk and his speech was good. But his memory was affected.'

Jamie's grandmother, Betty, nursed her husband until his death and the whole family was desperately saddened when he finally passed away. It was not that he had not had a good innings, Jamie reflected later, it was the cruel way the joys of life were taken away from him. He believed that no one deserved that sort of treatment and he grieved very deeply.

Jamie suffered again along with Jools when her father Maurice died in 1997 after a series of strokes and more than a decade of ill-health. Jamie was desperately upset as he struggled to comfort Jools. Her father was what Jamie described as a Stock Market person, a City broker. Jamie reckoned his life was just like a classic film story of the man with everything – an attractive model wife and three beautiful kids. Jamie says, 'Juliette was six when he had a stroke so she still has memories of her dad as this successful and confident high-flier with flash cars and a big house and not a care in the world. Overnight, it all disappeared. You rarely think about the future until it is too late. It all went pear-shaped and they had to move. They were suddenly not very well off but Jools's mother, Mrs Norton, still managed. She became very protective and she brought up three lovely girls.

'When I first met Jools's dad, I was a bit scared,' says Jamie. 'He was a 55-year-old grown man, but I had never met and really got to know a disabled person before. I thought the best thing I could do was just to talk to him like a mate.'

It remains one of the wisest moves of his young life. Jamie's instinctive decision to confront this awkward social problem head on was greatly appreciated by Jools and her family. They had seen too many of their former so-called friends mysteriously drift away from poor, stricken Maurice. When he was no longer any use to them in business and somewhat difficult to communicate with, Jools's mother found out exactly who her husband's real friends were.

Jamie simply ignored Maurice's sad disability and, with his openness and total lack of pretension, he made a great friend. Jamie said, 'I didn't go through anything like Jools went through with her dad. It more or less ruined her childhood. Jools was forced to live through her father's cruel illness almost throughout her growing up.'

Jools says, 'I remember Mum telling us what a stroke was, although I was not interested at the time. I thought it was something that would pass. But I can honestly say I had two fathers. There was the one who lived with us before the stroke and the one after.'

Although her father learned to walk and talk again, he never fully recovered after two more strokes, before the fatal one in October 1997. Jools says, 'Jamie was never embarrassed. Any other boy would have run a mile from scenes like that but he was brilliant.'

Jools and Jamie had really begun going out properly together when they were 17 and, two years later, Jamie asked Maurice for his daughter's hand in marriage. His reply was, 'You're a lovely chap, Jamie. I couldn't be more happy about you, but I think you're a bit young.' Jamie wondered exactly what that meant but, before he could work it out, Maurice gave the go-ahead. 'Of course you can marry her.'

'That was on New Year's Eve, when I was 19 and skint,' Jamie recollects fondly. 'I was working as a pastry chef and earning a couple of hundred quid a week. I'd just moved from the country to London and I was living in a tiny studio flat. Jools was modelling but she wasn't earning regularly so we had about £20 a week between us to live on.

'I couldn't afford to buy her a ring for three years. I know it sounds pathetic, but I didn't have any cash until then. And then when I did, I drew a picture of a ring and gave it to a jeweller in Hatton Garden who gave me a good deal. But by the time I got the ring, Maurice had died.

'Nearly four years ago, on Christmas Eve, Jools and I went to put some flowers on his grave. It was raining but I thought, I'll do it here, so I re-proposed to her. At the time, I thought it was a big sparkler, but it's not really.'

The experience of the two tragic deaths is one of the bonds that binds Jamie and Jools together. Each has been very much there for the other when they have most needed it. Friends say they sometimes seem almost telepathic and certainly their habit of suddenly coming out with the same thought at almost the same time has become something of a family joke. 'We do feel the same about an awful lot of things,' says Jamie. 'Often we communicate what we're thinking with just a look or a slight nod and we know what we mean but I don't think anyone else does. I often think how lucky I am to have met her. If I had left school a little earlier, or if she hadn't come to the sixth form, then someone else might have met her and be in love with her now. I don't even like to think about that.'

The River Café is in Thames Wharf, Hammersmith, West London, on the bank of the Thames where diners can eat outside under white canopies which proclaim the restaurant's name in fancy lettering. Opposite, standing imposingly on the other bank of the Thames, is the huge Harrods furniture depository building.

The River Café is a very attractive-looking restaurant tucked in between offices and smart flats. In the final years of the twentieth century, it was very much the fastest-rising restaurant in London in terms of popularity with a growing reputation for fine food. Jamie Oliver decided it was time to move on, and The River Café became his next target.

While he was working at Neal Street, Jamie was completely knocked out when he read *The River Café Cook Book*. 'I thought it was amazing,' he says. His eyes were out on stalks and he decided that that was the place to move to. It was not that he was unhappy where he was, but Jamie is an eternally restless young man who never wants to let the grass grow under his feet. He wanted to be at the cutting edge of culinary success and he wanted it quickly. So he launched a full-scale Jamie Oliver charm assault on The River Café.

It took him some sustained pestering. He reckons he made more than ten phone calls before he talked his way into a job there.

'It was not that I was unhappy, because I was very happy,' he told friends at the time. 'I just feel, when you're young you have to bang in the experience as quickly as you can.' He did not want to be regarded as a 'one-trick pony', he wanted to be London's best chef and he knew that meant gaining as wide a variety as possible of top-class experiences. So it was with regret and reluctance that he made the decision to move. 'But I will always move on until I am older and much more settled,' he says. It was simply that The River Café felt like a natural progression and it felt like the right time to make it.

If he had been happy before, he was in heaven now. Jamie loved The River Café. After his coaching from the charismatic Gennaro, Jamie affirms, 'My other big break in life was meeting Rose Gray and Ruth Rogers of The River Café and working for them. They are very inspirational people. They are not cliché chefs, not "cheffy" in the slightest. They have passion and they are not at all pretentious about their food.'

He loved being a part of the fashionable eaterie. He was much less impressed by the constant flow of celebrities who passed through than by the process of pushing back new frontiers of excitement in the kitchen. There was an uplifting team spirit about the place that really enthused the young chef. One of his favourite times of the week was Sunday morning when he used to prepare a massive pan of scrambled eggs for about 20 staff. It would be served with slices of grilled ciabatta, cut nice and thick and rubbed with garlic. Jamie's Australian pal Bender was on hand to finely chop some red chilli.

'We all tucked in, in true River Café style,' said Jamie.

Happy days indeed. He loved being a part of a thrusting young team. His sporting interests had never been firmly focused on the football field, but he reckoned that being a member of The River Café first team was as exciting for him as joining the Arsenal midfield would have been. Had he been gifted the footballing talent, that is. There was a buzz about the kitchens that turned Jamie on and he became famous for arriving for work early for his shift, and often being last to leave. 'It's corny, I know, but my dad always reckoned that the more you put in, the more you get out,' said Jamie. 'And that is exactly how I have found it in life. If I get a bit bored and start taking things for granted and cutting corners, I soon find that I am not stimulated and I am not enjoying myself. I get like a car that is not firing on all cylinders.'

Jamie and The River Café were exactly right for each other. One pretentious food critic burbled late at night about the 'synergy' between them and Jamie smiled genially as if he knew or cared what the guy was on about. To him, it simply felt as if he had become a key member of the first team and it felt fantastic.

Happily, the feeling was heartily mutual. 'Jamie is one of the most talented chefs we have,' says Ruth Rogers, who was not in the least bit surprised by his massive subsequent success because he was always smart, curious, ambitious and hard-working. She says no one at the restaurant harboured any resentment at his sudden rise to fame and fortune. 'Not at all. Everyone here is really happy and really proud for him.'

And head chef Arthur Pott-Daw agreed. 'Jamie is a lovely guy, bubbly. Everyone loves him.'

'I think it is in his blood to be a cook,' says Rose Gray. 'I feel sure he will be one of the country's great chefs.'

Jamie was starting to think so, too, but at the time he was still enjoying his education. 'In 1997, I went to Florence with the team from The River Café. It wasn't exactly a holiday because it was really supposed to be work. But it turned into sheer pleasure. We went to source ingredients and to taste the new season's olive oil. We stayed in different vineyards all over the place and went down into cellars that were hundreds of years old with loads of history and we saw little secret compartments where walls had been blocked off to the Germans during the War. I was blown away by the sensational simplicity of the food. It was very rustic with lots of white truffles all over the gaff and brilliant oil. Food in the households was fantastic – seven-course lunches and dinners and wine with everything. It seemed to me that very often the best cooking in Italy is done at home. Because despite having good ingredients the restaurants often got it wrong and many times when we ate out I was not in the least bit impressed.'

But there was the occasional heart-stopping highlight that Jamie will always remember. He was absolutely knocked out by one culinary find. 'By a complete fluke, I discovered one terrific dish in a grotty little café in Florence. It was a really simple salad with artichokes and shaved parmesan that is in my book,' said Jamie.

Chapter Four

Discovery

Jamie Oliver's discovery by the all-powerful medium of television for the delight of a vast worldwide audience is sure to become the stuff of small-screen legend in years to come. He is one of those very rare people who behave identically whether or not the TV cameras are rolling and his rise to fame and fortune was as sudden as it was unexpected. Jamie was sublimely uninterested when he first heard a TV crew was filming a look at life inside the restaurant. Despite what you might think or have heard to the contrary, Jamie Oliver had no more ambitions to become a television personality than the next man. If he had a long-term aim, it was to live in the country with the lovely Jools, raise lots of children and run a country pub or restaurant with the very same attention to quality and detail that his father taught him. Come to think of it, that is still Jamie's long-term ambition. Television just popped up in that arrogant, all-important way it tends to, and side-tracked Jamie to stardom.

It was when he was working at The River Café as a sous-chef that Jamie was first talent-spotted. He had been larking about playfully in the background of a BBC documentary being made about Ruth Rogers and Rose Gray called *Christmas at The River Café*. He was just being himself, chatting and working and refusing to be over-awed by the cameras in the way that normally sane people frequently are, but he must have made an impression.

'They filmed me quite a lot,' says Jamie. 'I think it was because I was really busy. They kept asking me what I was doing and because I was so rushed off my feet, the camera did not really bother me, so I did not come over as too shy. I never thought they would use any of it but they had all these 45-second snippets and they used them all the way through.'

Of course, most people would have turned instantly into a gibbering wreck at the prospect of being given a chance to audition on TV. Even Jamie admits that most chefs are born performers and show-offs, so this was the sort of opportunity that does not drop in your lap very often in a lifetime. Jamie knew perfectly well what he was doing, but he did not think anyone apart from a few catering chums and most of the members of his adoring family would get the joke. It was just a laugh to Jamie, showing off on television. But the punchline arrived on the day after transmission.

The day after the documentary went out, the phone at The River Café was ringing off the hook with offers, although, modestly, Jamie thought they were all from mates messing around. To be absolutely accurate, quite a few of the calls *were* from mates messing around. One even did a very bad Delia Smith impression ordering him to keep his smart-Alec style out of the superior world of the television kitchen. But rather more seriously, Jamie received no fewer than four firm offers to go into television and the one he accepted made him a star. That was in 1997, and he was just 21 years old.

'Guys in the kitchen were chucking food at me, so it was hard to take anything seriously,' he recalled afterwards. 'But I suddenly realised that one caller was using words like "commission" and "pilot" which were far too intelligent for my mates to know.'

That particular call he eventually took seriously was from Pat Llewellyn at Optomen Television. She is best known as the woman who invented that other innovative television cooking success story, *Two Fat Ladies*, a quirky hit featuring Clarissa Dickson-Wright with Jennifer Paterson, two genuine characters who combined brilliantly on screen. Pat knows a potential television star when she sees one and she instantly loved Jamie's cheeky, chirpy style and his confident lack of shyness in front of the frequently inhibiting camera.

But more than that, Pat Llewellyn's parents had run a restaurant in Wales and she had worked as the assistant producer on Sophie Grigson's 1992 cookery series *Grow Your Greens, Eat Your Greens*. With the benefit of 20-20 hindsight, Grigson says, 'Looking back at it, Pat was brilliant at what she did. She has a rare talent to spot people who are going to come across well on television. She is quite firm to work with, but very diplomatic. She allows her presenters to flourish by supporting, rather than intimidating, them.'

Llewellyn's success with the *Two Fat Ladies* had already given her massively increased clout within the industry, and she had this nagging idea for a cookery programme that would switch on a great untapped audience of younger viewers who largely would not be seen dead watching Anthony Worrall Thompson or Delia Smith. 'There are an awful lot of young people who just stick their food in the microwave and can't even boil an egg,' she said.

She was already searching for the right presenter and said, 'I must have looked at 20 or 30 people, but nobody was quite right. Then I saw Jamie on telly in one of The River Café programmes. He seemed very intent on what he was doing but he looked like he would have credibility with blokes.' She arranged to meet Jamie at her local café and was instantly impressed. He did not stop talking throughout the whole lunch. She decided he was absolutely perfect. Here was a man who was completely passionate about food who was living exactly the sort of life younger viewers could and surely would identify with. Jamie's modern London lifestyle was an advertising man's dream. It encapsulated all the images of sex appeal and success that would surely prove irresistible. His cool flat, his friends, his beautiful girlfriend, his attractive family would all look perfect on television and they all became part of the package. Even his spiral staircase, which was later to drive some exasperated viewers to distraction as they wondered at the number of times he plummeted to his door.

Amazingly, Jamie Oliver held out against making the big leap into television for a long time. Working in a busy London restaurant is hardly a rest cure and most 21-year-olds working long shifts and 'skint', as Jamie puts it, would have jumped at the chance of stardom and a fat pay cheque.

But his feet were firmly on the ground and, even if fame and fortune was clearly being dangled in front of him, he was certainly no pushover. Jamie did not have the remotest problem with being made rich and famous, but if it was going to happen to him, he was determined to do it his way. Even at 21, Jamie had already thought long and hard about his long-term future. He wanted to work with the best people, get all the experience he could and then open his own restaurant with him doing the cooking and his beloved Jools running the front of house. He also wanted to write a book and had already started this project some years earlier.

When the television company approached him, he was determined not to rush headlong into it and be moulded into something he was not. He had very definite ideas about the kind of television show he wanted to be involved with. He had some very strong and, in some cases, entirely unprintable ideas about some of our best-known television chefs and he was not prepared simply to take the money and allow himself to be manipulated into doing something third- or even second-rate. He definitely did not want to 'look stupid' or just become some kind of ghastly flash in the pan. Instinctively, he felt that there were probably more than enough chefs on our television screens already but he would have a go if, and only if, the programme-makers wanted him as he really was.

It was an unusual, high-risk strategy. Optomen could easily have waved goodbye to the rather cocky young man with attitude and found another hopeful from the many thousands queuing around the block. Producers do not like unknown performers who have awkward, strongly-held ideas before they have even begun working with them. They are used to unknown figures who are so desperate to get on television that they would do a fan dance in a bathtub full of custard in the first series. Generally, it is only after the malleable, co-operative unknown is transformed into an overnight sensation that he or she starts to insist on the best tables in all the restaurants and gets his or her agent to ring *Hello!* magazine to start an auction for exclusive coverage of a new hairdo. Jamie was not at all like that.

Instead, Jamie wrote his own detailed proposal for the show, built around the question, 'What does a 21-year-old chef cook at home?' Of course, it was a question that he certainly felt best equipped to answer, but he was determined to do it honestly. Optomen and the BBC liked it as much as they liked him and the series got the go-ahead, although it wasn't without problems.

At first, Jamie simply loathed and hated the name. 'Someone at the BBC came up with the title *The Naked Chef*,' he says. 'When I wrote my original proposal, I said something about stripping food down to its bare essentials, and from those two words they came up with this name for a porno king.

'When they first told me I was going to be called The Naked Chef, I said, "No way. What is my mother going to say?" I was scared because I knew the name was gagging for trouble, just asking for it. But once I got over the shock factor, I was quite pleased because it does mean what I want it to mean. And it is extremely distinctive.'

Mind you, when you consider some of the alternatives, Jamie can think himself fortunate. An earlier idea was to call the show *Forking Gorgeous*. But calling yourself The Naked Chef did encourage every journalist and chat show host to think they were being stunningly original by asking Jamie why he had got his clothes on. To his eternal credit as a human being, he refrained from hitting a single one of them.

Nowadays, Jamie believes, 'It has actually turned out to be a good thing, because I was so paranoid about the cheesy name that it became all the more important that the show was honest and reflected my character. My philosophy on food is all in favour of simple flavours. I am not into elaborate architectural structures with dribbles of this and that or in things that look a lot better than they taste. I don't want to cook poncey restaurant food, but I do want to prepare and demonstrate lots of good simple grub.'

From the very start Jamie was implacably determined to be down to earth at all times. He insisted, '*The Naked Chef* is all about getting rid of the bullshit in cooking. Chefs currently enjoy a status somewhere up there with pop stars. They're too busy sitting down at your table, showing off or having spats to cook. I wrote down what I wanted the show to be, with my real friends and family in my home, not on a set. I wanted to be seen going down to the markets, picking the stuff up, groping it, smelling it – cheeky shopping. It is easy to go to a restaurant and get pukka food, at a price. When you are at home, you still want the flavours and the good ingredients, but you want to cut out the bullshit. An idiot could do the recipes.'

Ominously, Jamie predicted, 'It really upsets me when a restaurant is fashionable and yet the food is not any good. You wonder how much the chef is in the kitchen cooking. There is no way I will end up as a celebrity chef. I am just myself. I am not putting on an act. I think that is crap.'

Pat Llewellyn could see that Jamie Oliver was that rare thing, a natural television performer. Those who know him best say there is almost no change in his behaviour off or on camera. He is not so much supremely confident and completely unfazed by the presence of cameras, he simply ignores them and is able to remain almost always his usual easy-going self.

Admittedly, he did try to be very much more 'BBC' for his first attempt. They made a pilot programme with Jamie speaking in 'cheesy lingo' straight into the camera but it did not work. 'I sounded all polite, like I was talking to your mum,' said Jamie, but the result was awful because Jamie was not being anything like himself. He said, 'We had to chuck it away which was £65,000 gone.'

Apart from simplifying restaurant cooking to make it work at home, Jamie was also adamant that

young Jamie gets a feel for his new hat at the Time Out Food and Drink Awards.

© Rex Features

Above: The Cricketers pub in Clavering, Essex, run by Jamie's dad, Trevor. Jamie spent much of his childhood at the pub, where he started helping out in the kitchens aged eight

© Rex Featur

Below: An ambitious Jamie was eventually to have his own chain of restaurants.

© Rex Featur

bove: Launching the video of his show *Pukka Tukka*. © *Rex Features*

elow: A taste of success. Jamie sampling his own book, *Jamie's Great Britain*, in Germany.

© *Rex Features*

Jamie and Jools first met at school, aged 17 and 16 respectively. The couple have been together ever since.

© Rex Featur

Jamie's interests extend beyond the kitchen. Playing the drums in his band, Scarlet Division, and catching some waves in Newquay.

© *PA Photos and Rex Features*

Right: An ecstatic Jamie and Jools on their happy day in 2000. Jamie designed the menu for the reception, using only ingredients that were in season at the time.

© *Rex Features*

Below: Jamie and Jools were delighted to welcome their new baby, Poppy Honey Rosie Oliver, into the world in 2002.

© *Rex Features*

family man.

bove left: Jamie, Jools and a one-year-old Poppy Honey with baby Daisy Boo Pamela
liver in 2003. © *Rex Features*

bove right: A boy to add to the brood: Buddy Bear Maurice Oliver was born in 2010.
© *Rex Features*

elow: The happy parents in 2009 with Petal Blossom Rainbow Oliver. © *Rex Features*

Above: The never-ending pasta-making machine! Lovely jubbly.

© *Rex Featur*

Below: Jamie's success in the kitchen has made him a household name and the go-to chef when you're in need of a solid recipe.

© *Rex Featur*

he wanted it to look as though he wasn't trying too hard, as though cooking was something that anyone and everyone could do.

'I didn't want to work on a television set and be the kind of chef dressed in whites putting a piece of cod on to a pile of mashed potato. I wanted the cameras in my house and I wanted people to see the food being enjoyed by my friends and family. Cooking is not all about pretty bowls and passing food around. Sometimes it is just putting it in the middle and letting everyone dig in. Food should be practical. I loathe the idea of programmes that are all about toffee-nosed people with lots of cash sitting around at their dinner parties boasting about how rich they are.

'As I see it, the food that I show on television is not for some ghastly sort of tasteful élite. It is for Bob from Bognor or Bill the plumber and blokes on building sites. It is for real people who are prepared to accept that one of the most marvellous things about food is that it is a great leveller. We all have to eat it and I reckon when you're enjoying a meal with someone you should not be giving them any sort of ear-ache about what a big noise you have become. I believe there is a basic feeling of equality when you sit down and share a table with someone. For as long as that meal lasts you should never sit and list all your possessions or your achievements. Nobody likes a big-head. You should share the occasion and do your level best to make the people you are sharing the meal with enjoy it as much as they can as well.

'In my programme, I also wanted to get down the shops, down the markets and get the feel of the ingredients. I was determined to show that when chefs eat at home, they don't make dishes with coulis this and reduced that. They take normal ingredients and make them more tasty. My job is to get people excited. I have fantastic dinner parties at home that don't cost much. That is the kind of cooking I do on my show.'

Jamie knew there was a danger in what he was doing, that if he was not very careful the TV people could make him 'look like a complete and utter cock'. But he trusted Pat Llewellyn and he fought his corner every step of the way to the screen.

'I knew it had to be honest, that it had to show me just being myself,' he says, 'because I can't act and if I tried to behave like someone else it would have looked totally phoney. Let's face it, at that time nobody really needed another TV chef!

'I was determined to show the cooking as near to the real time it takes to prepare things as we could get. The camera work is very fluid and it can be a bit jumpy. But can you imagine what it is like to work at that speed? I knew I could only do it if I was being myself and if we did everything in about five takes. It is impossible to get very excited, it really slows it down. That programme has a massively honest time-scale. You won't see another cookery programme where the chef is reaching into the fridge, peeling things or chopping everything up. Nothing is ever prepared in my programme so in that respect it is all done in real time. The only things we go back for are close-ups.'

In fact, Jamie offered far more than a cookery lesson with that first series of *The Naked Chef*. He served up his whole life on a plate on the screen. His close friends, his girlfriend Jools and even his family were put under the spotlight. It wasn't so much a simple cookery show, it was a throbbing real-life soap opera and all the more entertaining than the usual fare from Walford or Weatherfield. This was young. This was glamorous. This was more like *Dallas* or *Dynasty* at the height of their fame and popularity. It showed the viewers a glimpse of London that was still swinging with vibrant energy as attractive young people enjoyed their food.

Jamie thought long and hard before he exposed himself and his family and friends to this massive intrusion into their private lives. He was most concerned about the impact on Jools. He knew that with her appearance she, of all people, would look simply gorgeous on television, just as she does in real life. But he was also concerned that it was possible the fame could change their relationship. Jamie might not have earned too much academic success at school, but he does possess an undeniable street smartness. And he remains deeply unimpressed by the tedious, transitory mantle of celebrity. 'Most famous people are so far up their own backsides they don't know what day it is,' was the comment from one of Jamie's country friends about the movers and shakers of London town. And after just a few months' exposure to the world of air-kissing and agents, he was inclined most heartily to agree.

But after adding up the pros and cons, and talking at length to his mum and dad, and at even greater length to Jools, he decided to leap on board the tiger of television and ride it for all it was worth. He knew that *The Naked Chef* was not going to be some obscure, down-market student advice show, demonstrating how to make the most of a kitchen bereft of anything but pasta and a tin of corned beef. This was going to be food being fun and all delivered by sexy young Jamie who looked so much like a rock star it was no surprise to anyone to discover that he had his own band.

Jamie talked in the unpretentious, accessible tones of a genuine lad. He didn't have a script, he just had oodles of endless enthusiasm and a vocabulary full of words like 'pukka' and 'clobber' and 'malarkey', which were swiftly picked up everywhere in the country where they had previously been totally unfamiliar. His bish-bash-bosh style of cookery spurned any thought of carefully measuring out quantities of ingredients. There was no controversy about whether grams really had taken over from pounds and ounces in Jamie's kitchen because he didn't use either. Jamie measured his amounts in handfuls and quickly established himself in his TV kitchen as not so much 'hand ons' as 'hands in'. He relied on his taste buds to tell him when meals were 'pukka', and he encouraged his followers to do the same.

He slid speedily down that trendy spiral staircase and viewers started to take notice in their millions. It could easily have turned people against him, a sort of 'watch my television series, buy my books and you, too, can have the smart flat, the gorgeous girlfriend, the impossibly trendy friends ... and play in a rock band'.

Did the public hate him for that? By some miracle they didn't. As that first series unfolded, his popularity grew and he quickly became the television cook everyone loved, even other chefs.

Yet it was certainly high-risk television. As the series opened, Jamie was asked by journalists about how he faced up to the likely prospect of being chased down the streets by nubile young girls anxious to sample much more than his roast lamb. Didn't he worry about the thought that designers would be desperate to clothe his lean 6ft 1in frame in their latest creations and he would be on the A list for every party. Before it arrived he simply couldn't believe in the concept of fame. 'What do I know?' he said. 'I'm just a chef.

'It's just me making dishes at home which anyone can cook, without having to spend all night in the kitchen,' said Jamie. 'Roping my mates in to help with the show stops me from getting nervous. Juliette thinks it is all great but she is determined to stay out of the kitchen. In the six years that I have known her, she has cooked three meals and, quite frankly, they have all been pretty horrible. I am enthusiastic for her to carry on and I have tried to sort her out. But it is easier for me to do all the cooking and washing up. It is quite fair really because she does all the washing.

'I got involved with choosing the music and I wanted the roving camera work. I thought we could do for TV cooks what the *Blair Witch Project* did for film. I only wanted to do what I wanted to do. And I wanted to keep it real. Even though I was only a young boy, I had a lot of integrity; we didn't do crappy, shallow food.'

It was more like a fly-on-the-wall documentary than a conventional cookery programme, as Patricia Llewellyn wisely allowed her charismatic young subject free reign to introduce himself. 'Cooking has got to be a laugh. It's gotta be tasty. It's gotta be fun,' he enthused at length. And thanks to the natural flair of Jamie Oliver and the perceptive skills of the programme-maker, that is exactly how it looked.

His first leg of lamb was attacked and caressed as physically as if he were making love to a deliciously grateful woman. He rubbed herbs all over the surface and enthused 'lovely jubbly' as he prepared a meal for fellow chefs. The vigour and energy with which he stuffed herbs into holes cut in the joint was a real surprise.

'Just shove it in the gaps,' he grunted with effort, in a scene that made some viewers wince and others drool.

Rock music swept over the feast as the young food experts voted with their experienced taste buds and declared Jamie's meal a sensation before enjoying a game of table football together.

Jamie Oliver was instantly seen as the ultimate lad. He was kind and caring, streetwise but sensitive, and the enthusiasm with which he prepared his food was undeniably infectious. He was completely different to other TV personalities like Anthony Worrall-Thompson or Ainsley Harriott. Jamie was a real guy with a real life and food clearly played a very important part in it.

Jamie was so inventive as well. He was not above grinding up a box of Maltesers to mix into ice cream. His sister Anna's hen night was an inspired choice of subject. 'My sister is coming round with ten leery ladies,' said Jamie. 'It is not going to be very quiet.'

And, best of all, he never appeared to take himself too seriously. 'The TV series is great. I don't have to try very hard. I open my mouth and it just comes out.'

Jamie made sure there was plenty of his favourite music and loved being noisily backed by Toploader. He was already so 'right on' he came out with the perfect lines often without coaching from programme-maker Pat.

'Free range, they've gotta be free-range eggs,' said Jamie with sincerity that was patently obvious to the viewers, 'because they look better, they taste better and I don't like the idea of battery hens.'

Jamie's Uncle Allen arrived with his kids to be entertained. 'It's Uncle Allen who looks like Cliff Richard but he can't sing and Cliff has never been married while Uncle Allen has had three wives,' said Jamie.

But when he turned up he did look a tiny bit like Cliff Richard, so we could all see what Jamie meant. They seemed to enjoying eating the ravioli an awful lot more than they did playing Twister.

His mortar and pestle became so popular they were like early co-stars for Jamie. Viewers asked where to find them and Jamie advised, 'You can normally get them from every Thai, Indian or Oriental deli which are in most big cities now. They cost around £13 to £18. It is probably the best gadget you can buy in the world without a doubt,' said Jamie without even bothering to negotiate himself a percentage.

We saw Jamie in action with his band before he cooked them a particularly delicious-looking Thai green curry and we knew he was telling the truth when he admitted, 'I'm a cliché drummer, a little bit hyperactive, and I talk rubbish most of the time.'

Not that it was all plain sailing. The endless trips on his quick bannister ride downstairs were not always uneventful. 'I did once have an accident sliding down the spiral staircase,' he confessed later. 'When we were making the Christmas Special, the stairs broke and I had a bruise about four inches long on my behind!'

And an excursion to the seaside with his young cousins almost ended in a tantrum from Jamie. 'It was an absolute nightmare,' he groans. 'One of them is 12 and the other is 6 and they had their friends with them. They absolutely harassed me to the point of near tears. I felt as if I had been beaten up in a rugby match.'

Jamie clearly enjoyed himself massively while working on that blissfully innocent and largely unknown first series. 'Little gems of things quite literally just happen naturally in a day of filming. And that to me is what the series is all about. It is massively spontaneous.'

He certainly seemed to be living his job as he confided at one point, 'The other night, I was dreaming about whether I should use red onions or white onions while cooking a roast. And it used to be naked women in *Baywatch* that filled my dreams. Now I dream about onions. It is because I am completely obsessed by food.'

Jamie's unique selling point seems to be his basic lack of guile. 'We really do have a dinner party in every episode but we can't show the end of the party because people often finish up completely plastered,' he admitted cheerily as the BBC publicity department collectively held its breath. His honest enthusiasm comes screaming out of the screen at you.

The Naked Chef was a hit right from the start and Jamie was too excited about it all to be bothered with any fake modesty. Or any real modesty, come to that. He said as the rave reviews flooded in and the viewing figures shot skywards, 'The secret about the programme is that it is real. I am not mincing around the house in chef's whites. It's pretty simple. It's me, at my house, with my friends and my family, having a laugh and cooking. The Jamie you get on telly is the Jamie you get in real life. *The Naked Chef* is about stripping down complicated restaurant food. It's just a lot of little tricks and short cuts and having a good time really. If you can get something that is accessible and that tastes fantastic, and if you can rip things up instead of having to chop them, or have handfuls of things instead of getting the scales out, then I am all for it.' Jamie was really warming to his theme by then as he articulated elegantly, 'Measuring things is a load of boring old bollocks.'

But people say a lot of strange things in the

heat of the moment. Jamie said later, 'I was 21 and I have learned a lot since then. If someone asked me to do that now, I would say "No". But at the time, all I knew was that it had to be different. I know I gave more than the average cooking programme. The viewers got to meet my best friends, my family, Jools, the in-laws, all sorts. But I think that is where cooking should be placed. It's not just food, it's socialising, it's mingling, it's having a laugh … when I talk about food I don't perform, I just get excited. Sometimes it's just bollocks.'

Jamie made bread specially for one show and looked as if he enjoyed every moment of it. He said it was very therapeutic kneading the yeast and flour together. Even at his young age, he realised he might be coming across like an 'old git' going on about how good it was to make bread, but he scarcely cared. 'Some boys like to put lowered exhaust pipes on their Ford Escort XR3is,' he smiled, 'but I like to make bread.'

Jamie was just naturally fresh and appealing on TV. And he didn't hand out any patronising advice for not crying while peeling onions; in fact, he said, 'I like to have a good cry at work,' with a frankness that endeared him even more to his growing army of female fans. And the way he squelched butter in his hands made younger viewers squeal with envy that their parents would never let them handle food like that.

Jamie was anxious never to analyse too closely why the shows worked. He thought that was very dangerous indeed. And when the famous BBC focus groups sat in judgement, he could hardly have been less interested. Jamie wanted to organise his television programmes with the same instinctive good taste and sensitivity that he organised his life. He followed his nose, his eye, his ear and, above all, his taste for the next delicious dish. But he never wanted to sit for hours contemplating his navel and trying to work out where he had gone right in case the magic formula disappeared as soon as it was identified. To be fair, when fiercely pestered, he did once say, 'The secret of my success, if there is one, is a little bit of luck, a little bit of passion and a little bit of knowledge! Everyone was always telling me it was going to be a young person's programme and I wanted it to be for everyone and it has got the biggest young and old-age pensioner following on BBC2.'

Unfortunately, filming in a real home had repercussions in Jamie's case, when real life intruded rather unpleasantly into the fantasy life of television. When a local teenage gang saw the cameras moving into Jamie's trendy studio flat in

East London, they did not head for Sainsbury's to stock up with vanilla pods. Instead, with a singular lack of imagination, they began to victimise and harass him. Things got so bad that even before the show was seen on television, Jamie moved to a new address in West Hampstead, North London.

Jamie says, 'This gang would constantly bang on the door and the windows and scribble graffiti on the walls. They were doing silly things like spray painting the windows. Then, one day, it got more serious. My computer got nicked from my flat and one day I found my car had a puncture. I took it to be fixed and the guy said I had six huge nails in the tyres. I had a Jeep at the time and the tyres cost about £250 each. I spent £750 replacing them and decided things had got stupid. It was just 13- and 14-year-olds who were bored.'

Jamie's dream car, in fact, is an Aston Martin, but he is more likely to be seen in the more practical Frontier Jeep. Generally, now, though, he gets round London on his scooter. 'I have had four of them so far and I am on my fifth. People keep nicking them and my insurance company think I am a liability. I have an extremely large padlock now, though!'

If he had been able to talk to those bored teenagers one to one, the chances are that Jamie could have won them over and converted them to watching and enjoying the show. He would happily have cooked for them all if they hadn't been so hell-bent on wrecking every bit of his life. When Jamie became concerned for Jools's safety, he knew it was time to give in gracefully and move on. And when a teenage girl was attacked by the gang at the end of the road, Jamie decided it was time to head for pastures new.

The remarkable thing is that as recently as April 1999, Jamie was still just 23 years old and totally unknown. But his life was about to change for ever. *The Naked Chef* was about to be launched on an unsuspecting public. Two months later, he was the hottest chef in town and he could no longer lurch round the markets chatting uninterrupted to the stallholders. Every time he went out, autograph hunters would appear as if by magic and, as he said, it took a bit of getting used to. Jamie spent many hours explaining to people that the catchy title did not mean that, in spite of the undoubted enthusiasm of female viewers, he was about to parade about his kitchen with no clothes on. The programme's title referred to his sublime ability to strip food down to its absolute basics.

The ratings were sensational for upmarket BBC2. *The Naked Chef* regularly pulled more than

5 million viewers to make it comfortably the most popular show on the channel and Jamie started to find out what it is like to be recognised everywhere you go. He refused to complain because he so desperately wanted the show to be a success and he had invested so much of his own life in it.

One of Jamie's most significant strengths is to have the courage of his convictions. When the BBC were forever urging him to shape the show to the youth market, Jamie flatly refused to be anything other than himself. Certainly, *The Naked Chef* was a hit with the young and beautiful but it was also popular with viewers of all ages. Jamie said perceptively for someone so young that he simply did not believe that old people only want to watch old people on television. And the number of pensioners who switch on to his show proves he was right. One 75-year-old female fan let her temperature rise so high when she met Jamie on a book tour in Leeds that she couldn't resist patting his bottom for 30 seconds. Jamie was astonished and somewhat embarrassed, but her 80-year-old husband did not seem to mind at all.

For a time, Jamie simply refused to let fame change his life. He continued to combine his job at The River Café with the television work and the book and all the promotional demands that followed the world's discovery of the charismatic cook from Clavering. He loved working at the exciting cutting-edge restaurant and, at first, he was fiercely determined to stay on there. He was determined not to let a little thing like television change his life that greatly. But it was a vain hope as, gradually, fan fatigue began to set in and the attention of admirers got in the way of his work in the restaurant. He handed in his notice in the autumn of 1999 as the Jamie Oliver success story seemed to be generating new chapters just about every day.

Jamie recalls the moment of decision as 'well upsetting'. Rose and Ruthie and his workmates had all become very close and supportive friends, 'beautiful people' as he called them, and he did not want to leave. But the power of celebrity is a frightening force and it simply began to get in the way of the everyday running of the restaurant. Jamie found it really embarrassing when waiters came running up with menus for him to autograph while everyone else was trying to serve the diners. He found it even more excruciating when he had to tell the waiters off for simply following the customers' demands.

Jamie said at the time that it was traumatic having to say goodbye to the 'friends who have become like family' at The River Café. He knew that the trendy eaterie had given him the finest platform for his television talents to be spotted in the first place and he was desperately reluctant to leave. He was frightened that without his highly enjoyable base in the real world he might flutter and die in the fickle world of television.

'I feel at home in The River Café,' he said. 'I can be the real me here. If I go I feel like the television me has taken over and I never really want that to happen.' But go he did because, whatever his anxious reservations, he knew that life for him had changed for ever.

His great and long-lasting ambition to own a restaurant of his own began to occupy his mind much more at this time. 'I feel like I am a lucky boy; I have got the book and the programme and that, but that's cosmetics, know what I mean? It's not where it all comes from. I feel something is missing without a restaurant of my own.

'I have this dream of a wonderful place just outside Cambridge where the atmosphere is just as exciting as the "bloody rustic" food,' said Jamie. 'I want to spend the time in the kitchens, not to be table-jumping with faces all the time, honest. But every time I start talking to money people, it frightens me off. Three years ago, getting money out of the bank was a nightmare. They just used to say, "Get lost." But now, they want to give you money – "Please, take it. Have a restaurant." It's scary and, in a way, it is worse and more worrying than being turned down.'

At the age of only 24, Jamie had become the unlikely heir to Delia Smith as the country's most popular television chef. *The Naked Chef* topped the BBC2 ratings for weeks. The book of the first series headed the bestseller lists for nearly six months before it was toppled by the book of the second series.

The two cooks could not be more different. On television, Delia is nothing if not self-controlled. By contrast, it's difficult to keep up with Essex-born Jamie. He rushes about his kitchen, he slides down his bannisters (polished for the purpose with Mr Sheen), he plays his drums, and the director adds to the high-octane 'yoof TV' feel of the show by swinging the camera about. And then there is his distinctive vocabulary. Littered with words like 'malarkey', 'pukka' and 'clobber', it is straight out of *The Lavender Hill Mob*. Where does he get it from?

'Everybody in Essex says "pukka",' he says with a puzzled expression.

The book was a natural offshoot of the series and Jamie is too full of confidence in his own ability to have second thoughts about putting his ideas on paper. 'Sure, experience means a lot,' he said. 'But the idea that you have got to have worked all over the world, under ten Michelin-starred chefs, for ten years, 18 hours a day before you can even pick up a menu, let alone write one, is bollocks! I could get someone off the street, teach 'em to make amazing pasta and in a month they could open their own amazing pasta place and get rave reviews.'

Jamie's book sold more than 350,000 copies in this country alone and was number one on the bestsellers list for more than four months. When he featured vanilla pods on his shows with the usual Oliver enthusiasm, the shops sold out. It was just like Delia and the cranberries. The book sold for £18 and Jamie received 45p per copy, which is rather less than the 10 per cent that writers usually get. But he didn't have an agent at the time and he was overawed by the whole process. He has moaned about the experience from time to time, but now he has an agent his book revenues are heading through the roof with the new books. Jamie prefers to put the deal behind him and insists, 'I don't like whingeing, I just make sure I don't make the same mistake twice.'

The book was not exactly a trouble-free experience. The Penguin copy-editors were baffled by some of Jamie's slang and tried to take it out of the book. It was 'What does wicked mean in this context?' and 'Why are we describing this food as pukka?' but Jamie stuck to his guns. He would not let them change his words and time has certainly proved him right.

But no one can say Jamie Oliver did not work hard for his book to succeed. He hurtled round the country – and, later, round the world – to promote his book with enormous energy given his punishing schedule. For example, in Ireland he had just 20 hours to spend in Dublin, but in that time he signed books and autographs almost non-stop and still said the next day that he wished he'd had more time to meet more of the booksellers and to have done more signings.

'I feel guilty,' he told an impressed reporter. 'I have only done half the job. There are still lots of people I didn't have time to meet. I am just thrilled when people buy my book. I put a lot of effort into trying to get it right but it is all wonderfully well worthwhile when someone who has really appreciated it comes up to say thank you. I just love it when they tell me how a particular recipe went down well at a particular occasion. It gives me a huge kick. That's why I do the job. Food is a basic need but it is also a fantastic aid to enjoying life. Sometimes people come up and say the lamb was the perfect way of celebrating an anniversary or a wedding or any happy occasion. They're so kind and grateful that it makes my job one of the best in the world.'

But hard work comes into it as well as good fortune. Jamie explained that he was absolutely determined to get his book to number one and he was seriously businesslike in his attempts to give his book every possible advantage.

'In London, if I have to start work at twelve o'clock I'll often leave an hour-and-a-half early and I'll go round all the bookshops I can and sign all the books I can find. You can get through an awful lot of books in an hour-and-a-half. All the booksellers have my mobile number and they can ring me when they have more stock in.'

Some observers wonder why he bothers so much. Jamie responds, 'I put a lot of work into the book and the TV series. I worked my arse off. It is hard to get to number one in the non-fiction charts and nobody was more surprised than me when I hit it. So now I am working really hard to keep it there. Do you know what I am up against? The *Star Wars* book, that's what.'

Naturally, in Britain it is hard for any television performer to please everyone. And almost as soon as the first wave of public enthusiasm had swept him to fame, the nit-picking attacks were being formulated. Reviewers swooped to sneer that Jamie was speaking 'Estuary English' which produced large gales of laughter from the man in question.

' "Estuary English" really makes me laugh,' he said. 'I don't live anywhere near an estuary and I don't know what kind of an accent I have got. I'm a country guy and my friends were country people and, like me, they were as common as muck. My mum used to tell me off for being common and say, "Why can't you speak properly?" and I would say "Introduce me to the Queen and I'll be polite, but when I'm relaxed I drop a couple of aitches." '

But the 'Mockney' accent did not prevent him from being invited to Number 10 Downing Street to cook for the Prime Minister. Jamie was surprised and a little daunted to receive the invitation from Tony Blair to come and cook for the PM and his opposite number from Italy.

'It was an honour,' said Jamie, but he had cooked for Tony Blair before at Ruthie's house so it was not quite the ordeal it might have seemed at the time. Jamie said, 'Tony wanted to prove to the Italians how much English food has improved and I cooked them a really swanky lunch.'

Of course, he was still extremely anxious for the

meal to be a success. He knew the Italian party would be well acquainted with the finest cuisine and he really went for it. He selected six bass and had the ricotta flown over especially from Naples. He chose all the vegetables and cheeses personally. Jamie made a ravioli for the Prime Ministers and stuffed it with the ricotta and added his favourite pecorino and some parmesan. The bass were outrageous he recalled later, 'so fresh they still had *rigor mortis*'. He filleted them, stuffed in herbs and roasted them over sliced potatoes and two sorts of mushrooms. The pudding comprised of five English cheeses served with apricots, peaches and figs.

Afterwards, he gave the Italian Prime Minister a copy of his book which appeared to go down well. Jamie felt Tony Blair was pleased with his efforts and later asked for a doggy bag for what was left of the potato dish.

Afterwards, Jamie said, 'Walking in the door of 10 Downing Street is about as cool as it gets. Tony Blair said, "You know, Jamie, I don't know how you do it. You have such a hard job." I had to laugh – his is the world's hardest job!

'Cherie said, "Oh you're the Naked Chef, but you've got your clothes on!" What does she expect? That I come to Number 10 with me knob out?'

The Naked Chef TV show and books have won

Jamie a huge and faithful army of fans. Even youngsters tell him that they have tried out some of his recipes. And, like the rest of us, he makes himself baked beans on toast when the cupboard is bare. Jools also keeps his head out of the clouds.

On top of the book's success, the TV show has made Jamie the first English chef to have his own programme on Italian television. France and Germany could be just around the corner. 'But Italy is more of an achievement than France,' says Jamie. 'While the French are proud of their food, the Italians are even prouder. Food is almost a religion in Italy and they squabble over every aspect of cooking. So for them to let an English boy into the market is amazing.'

Chapter Five

Patten to Oliver –
the TV Years

When Jamie Oliver exploded on to British television screens on 14 April 1999 with his first series, *The Naked Chef*, he was joining a long and illustrious line of celebrity television cooks.

Britain has always had an insatiable appetite for culinary activities on television, even though most of us nowadays watch cookery shows with take-aways perched on our knees. But how the cooking culture on screen and the personalities have changed since those heady days of television's early performers in the austere post-war years.

It was only just over 50 years ago that cooking made its début on television, but what a difference

117

between that first TV cook – Marguerite Patten, still going strong at 84 – and today's newest recruit, 26-year-old Jamie Oliver.

Before making her first television appearance in 1947, Marguerite had been guiding the nation through rationing on the radio. In her *Five-Minute Kitchen Front* talks on the Home Service, she taught housewives how to make 'mock duck' from cooking apples and sausage meat and gave handy hints on what to do with dried egg.

Her first television broadcast, from Alexandra Palace, was hardly ground-breaking – eight minutes on making doughnuts – but she was in at the beginning of what has become a massive television phenomenon with millions of pounds to be made by the successful star chefs. Amazingly, considering the plethora of chefs on the box and new ones queuing to become the next star, Marguerite still has her place in the spotlight. Last year, she was involved with the Channel 4 series *The 1940s House*, advising on the correct food for wartime Britain and recently published her latest book, *Marguerite Patten's Century of British Cooking*. She was also back on the radio with her own regular series, this time on Radio 4 and based on her book.

Marguerite is clearly remembered fondly and her advice and expertise over the years has been respected, but since those rather genteel early days there have been dozens of chefs trying to make it on the telly – only a handful instantly spring to mind as memorable and even fewer have had a lasting influence on the way Britain cooks and eats. Most, while they may have kept the British public entertained, haven't infiltrated the real British kitchen in any serious way.

In Marguerite's day, of course, information was the buzz word. Eight minutes on doughnuts proves the point. Today's telly chef could have created a five-course dinner and washed up in that amount of air time.

While Marguerite Patten was more a utility than a celebrity cook, the rotund and bewhiskered Philip Harben, around at the same time, was famously larger than life. He was memorable for his gentlemanly delivery, love of British food and trademark stripy apron and was probably television's first true culinary personality.

How difficult it must have been to break into television as a cook in those early days. Harben, though, was the ideal character to make it. Colourful, confident and enthusiastic, he was born into a theatrical family – his father was the classical actor Hubert Harben, and his mother, Mary Jerrold, won fame for her role in *Arsenic and Old Lace*.

During the war, his ambitions to become a pilot were thwarted following an eye injury and, instead, he joined the Royal Air Force catering division. When he was demobbed, he approached the BBC and said he wanted to be involved with food programmes. His career took off instantly and he was soon presenting weekly shows on radio and television, writing books and making personal appearances to packed houses around the country.

The era of the celebrity chef had arrived, ushered in by a man who went on to have an illustrious 20-year broadcasting career until his death in 1969. But back in the 1950s he was billed simply as *The Man in the Kitchen*, and when he began in 1953 he used to cook on screen with his family's rations. So if he burned the joint on television there would be no Sunday lunch for the Harben family. Philip Harben's sense of humour sadly did not extend to allowing himself to be made fun of. He famously walked out of a recording of *The Benny Hill Show* in 1955 when he did not like the script. He said at the time, 'They submitted a sketch to me which I considered degrading. It seemed devised to make me appear professionally incompetent. I was supposed to be half-tight and the whole thing indicated that I could not cook. That is no joke to me.' Somehow, it is hard to conceive of Jamie Oliver having that reaction if he was appearing on a comedy show.

By that time, of course, there were other pretenders to the throne, notably the inimitable Fanny and Johnny Craddock who were nipping at Harben's heels. She was strident, bossy and organised in a Hartnell ballgown; he cowered in the background in his tuxedo, clutching a glass of half-decent Hock. When they moved from BBC's *Kitchen Magic* to ITV to open up *Fanny's Kitchen* in the late '50s, it was a television sensation. They changed overnight from the BBC's formal Phyllis and John Craddock, the *bon viveur* husband-and-wife cookery team, to ITV's more relaxed and infinitely simpler Fanny and Johnny.

Despite the fact that writers like the remarkable Elizabeth David had been cooking up a revolution in real kitchens with exciting revelations about Mediterranean food and French country cooking since the early '50s, that wasn't the kind of food that made its way on to television screens.

Fanny and Johnny, and their classic French approach to cooking, dominated the television scene for what seemed like an age with series like the 1969 offering for the BBC, *How to Give a Dinner Party*. In those days balsamic vinegar, sun-dried tomatoes and fusion cooking were light years away and the Craddocks' style remained fussy and elaborate – hardly in step with David's 'omelette and a glass of wine'.

Fanny was all about entertainment and, when she took a break from harassing Johnny, her ambition seemed to be to turn women into perfect cook-hostesses, an aim curiously out of step as the Swinging Sixties and Women's Lib took hold.

So while Elizabeth David was truly changing the way Britons ate and turning on the middle-classes to the simple joys of food, Fanny was still offering recipes for *carré de porc aux marrons* followed by gâteau St Honoré.

Even as late as 1970, in one of their many cookery books, Fanny and Johnny were encouraging ladies to treat their next dinner party – or indeed any occasion where food and people met – like a battle, with the kitchen as the battle ground.

Whatever would she have made of Jamie's pukka tucker, mate?

After Fanny and Johnny, the man who perhaps best embraced the 'food is entertainment' ethos, bringing a new and more relaxed style to a television audience hungry for more, was the all-singing, all-dancing Galloping Gourmet, Graham Kerr – a cook and a showman who, in his own words, pursued 'hedonism in a hurry'.

He raced around the studio like a man high on senna pods and, in a way, he was the Jamie Oliver of his day, the first screen cook to put food and sex together. It was a winning recipe. Tall, good-looking and charming, he seduced his female audience with his smooth banter and ready smile, but it was the butter, cream and deep-fat frying that cemented his popularity. It was all quite outrageously flirtatious as he invited the audience to taste his food and plied them with wine, with wife Treena watching over him.

Delicious as it was, the food was almost a side issue as Kerr made television cookery into top-class entertainment. He's still going strong on American television but he's had something of a conversion. While his cooking style used to be rich and extravagant, he is now a guru of healthy eating, advocating strained non-fat yoghurt and de-alcoholised wine instead of the indulgences that endeared him to millions of female hearts.

In 1972, while recuperating after a near-fatal accident, Kerr began to experiment with a low-fat cooking style to help ease his family's stomachs while travelling at sea. The family, however, rebelled against Graham's first efforts with his 'caring' cuisine, claiming the food to be bland and unremitting. It was only after his wife had a heart-attack in 1986 that he refined his low-fat cuisine into something healthy and pleasurable.

He now heads the Kerr Corporation based in Mount Vernon, Washington, and extols his healthy-eating philosophy through many publications and his website *Wellness on the Web*. His television series, *Swiftly Seasoned*, airs on Public Service Broadcasting stations and his earlier shows are often reprised on the Discovery Channel.

If the Galloping Gourmet set the standard for the professional chef/entertainer, the rolling pin was grabbed enthusiastically by the loquacious Keith Floyd. For a decade from the mid-80s he dominated the television cooking scene and, just like Jamie, his style was totally original.

He made a sensational début with his first series, *Floyd on Fish*, broadcast on BBC2 in 1985. He was unmissable with his slightly 'frayed around the edges' looks, public school accent and totally irreverent attitude. Clutching the ubiquitous glass of red wine and taking regular hefty slurps, Floyd talked to ordinary people about food, life, love and fishing. He cooked on boats, up mountains and on beaches and generally had a high old time.

Just like Jamie, Floyd was nothing if not himself on screen. More series followed thick and fast – *Floyd on Food, France, Ireland, Italy, Oz*, as well as

Far Flung Floyd and *Floyd's American Pie*. A television career that began with six eight-minute cooking spots on HTV in 1981, when he ran a restaurant in Clifton, continues today on Channel 5 with Floyd still to be spotted, windswept, atop a mountain range, clutching a glass and putting the world to rights.

Floyd's relaxed approach to just about everything couldn't have been more different from the style and precision of another great chef on the box around the same time – Anton Mosimann. Chalk and cheese springs to mind. Floyd becoming increasingly more expansive and eccentric on screen, while Mosimann, a perfectionist, quietly extolled the virtues of restraint. He championed the cause of natural food without added oil, butter, cream and alcohol. Mosimann was not a scintillating performer but he was a great cook and his audience respected that. His first series, *Cooking with Mosimann*, was broadcast in 1989 by the BBC, although he later took his innovative and healthy style of cooking over to Channel 4.

And then there is Delia. Her first appearance on television was before Jamie was born. And she's never been off it since. Allegedly making her very last series for the BBC, Delia has influenced the way people eat in Britain, both through her television appearances and her writing, more than any other cook.

In the early days of a 30-year television career, it was pâté, beef in beer and cheesecake that she offered to her adoring public. Now, when Delia says cranberries, sales go up 200% in one day; when she says she just loves capers, they fly off supermarket shelves. In fact, some stores assign teams of people to trawl through the list of ingredients she plans to use for her television shows, trying to spot the potential big sellers.

However, even the experts were caught short when Delia called a rather innocuous £10.95 omelette pan 'a little gem' in the first of her BBC2 series, *How to Cook*. It was hardly cutting-edge culinary technology, but Delia's public had to have it. The tiny Lancashire firm which made the pan went from threatening redundancies due to poor sales to taking on 15 extra staff virtually overnight. They sold 90,000 pans in four months and their annual sales rose from a modest 200 to 140,000.

Her books are never out of the bestsellers list, including her *Complete Cookery Course*, written almost 20 years ago. Series like the *Summer Collection* in 1993 and the *Winter Collection* in 1995 made her place in British culinary history guaranteed. In the '90s it was hard to go to a dinner party without sitting down to a Delia dish. Her books are said to be in 10 million British homes.

While Delia has been the undoubted queen of television cooks for the past two decades, in the past few years she has had some tough – and some not quite so tough – competition: Rick Stein; Gary Rhodes; Nigel Slater; Raymond Blanc; Gordon Ramsay; Antony Worrall-Thompson; Clarissa Dickson-Wright and Jennifer Paterson; Sophie Grigson; Ainsley Harriott; Hugh Fearnley-Whittingstall ...

Then there's *Masterchef* and all those cheerful guys and gals on *Ready Steady Cook!* and *Can't Cook, Won't Cook* – Brian Turner; Lesley Waters; Phil Vickery; Paul Rankin; Nick Nairn ... not forgetting the endless cookery slots on regional and daytime television and Ken Hom putting in an appearance every Chinese New Year on *This Morning*.

By the time Jamie Oliver stripped down to his essentials on 14 April 1999, he was diving into a stock pot already overflowing and, after all the hype, hardened viewers and keen cooks alike could be forgiven for thinking that yet another television chef was one too many. Particularly when his name seemed to be a gimmick – the 'Naked Chef'.

It gave *The Galloping Gourmet* and *Nutter in the Kitchen* (whatever happened to him?) a run for their money as the daftest cookery programme title ever.

And then there was his age. He was so young when the first series of *The Naked Chef* was screened. What could he possibly know about cooking that Delia and others had not told us before? How could anyone take him seriously?

We knew how to cook the perfect Christmas lunch (Delia); boil live lobsters (Rick); create 20 dishes from a potato, a packet of prawns and a carrot (*Ready Steady Cook!*) and feed a convent full of nuns (*Two Fat Ladies*).

The Naked Chef was bound to be a flash in the pan, a gimmick, here today and gone tomorrow. The suspicion that the whole concept of the show was the result of a TV executive brain-storming session was hard to shrug off. From the pre-publicity, before anyone had seen a frame of Jamie, it all seemed too good to be true. Essex wide-boy, young, pretty, sexy and he cooks. Bingo! Instant hit. But how wrong all the cynics were.

Endearing, funny, cheeky, cute, sweet. In his first show, he looked like a slightly scruffy choir boy, not a day over 14. There he was slashing into a leg of lamb, poking it with his fingers, getting his hands stuck into a bowl of butter and herbs and then sliding down the bannister of the spiral staircase at his flat and dashing out to buy fish – with the viewers trying to keep up with him.

All those cooks who stocked up on limes, lemon grass and anchovies with Delia, learned how to cook fish with Rick, and were turned on to great British classics by Gary Rhodes, suddenly had a new hero. The Essex boy with the looks of a cherub and the kind of sex appeal that made both teenage girls and their grannies want to take him home was the genuine article.

The viewers loved him and the BBC loved him even more because, as well as hooking the all-important younger viewers – the twenty- and thirty-somethings with money to spend – he also attracted the middle-aged, middle-class, Middle England audience on loan from Delia.

And he did it with a style not seen before on cookery programmes. Everyone was talking about Jamie Oliver and, as with many things in life, much of it came down to sex appeal.

With the best will in the world, the likes of Antony Worrall-Thompson, Rick Stein and Gary Rhodes just didn't have it, whereas Jamie just had to threaten to rub olive oil into an organic chicken to get the juices flowing. Curiously, blokes liked him, too. As he stood there in his kitchen, looking like he'd just got up, tearing open packets and bashing garlic around, cooking suddenly became achievable ... and sexy.

He was completely disarming and the critics were fulsome in their praise. The *Evening Standard* called him 'the hottest thing since chilli peppers'; the *Daily Telegraph* enthused, 'he looks like a rock star, sounds like a yob and cooks like an angel.'

Despite the naughty-but-nice title and the wonky camera angles, it was soon obvious that Jamie Oliver was about to become a major star and a very rich young man indeed.

As the word spread about *The Naked Chef*, the ratings climbed and the book Jamie wrote to accompany the series even knocked Delia off the top of the non-fiction bestsellers list. Delia gave him the thumbs-up. He admits that he thinks she's sexy.

So the Grande Dame and the young pretender have a mutual appreciation society going and, strange as it may seem, they have a lot in common. Although Delia's pushing 60 and Jamie's only just 26, their philosophies on cooking are very similar. Real food for real people.

While Delia achieves that with precision and attention to detail, taking away all a home cook's worries, Jamie achieves it with enthusiasm and flair. While Delia gives cooks confidence by telling them precisely what to do, Jamie says 'no worries'. Both of them are believed.

What they've both achieved is that rare thing in television cookery; they've succeeded in dragging viewers away from the television set and into the kitchen. Jamie's book to accompany the series flew off the shelves much like Delia's capers. Young people were suddenly presenting Peach, Proscuttio and Mozzarella Salad to their mates, just as their mothers served up Delia's Couscous with Roasted Vegetables and Thai Salmon in Filo Parcels.

But while Delia has a lifetime's experience to draw on, Jamie is still a baby by comparison. Even after two television series and two books, he's still only 26, an age when most young men have just about mastered the art of cooking frozen pizza. And beyond the fairytale success of his culinary, TV and publishing career, there are still several goals that the young Jamie has set his sights on.

Chapter Six

Married at Last

Always the man for the big occasion, Jamie finally formally proposed to Jools on Millennium Eve and the wedding was planned for 24 June 2000. By then, they had been an inseparable couple for seven years, so no one could accuse them of exactly rushing into anything. Jamie might look like a young Mick Jagger but he has never lived the pop star lifestyle with different girlfriends coming and going every night. Or wanted to. But there have been many young women who have decided it would be a cool challenge to try to come between Jamie and Jools.

When Jamie presented a prize at the National TV Awards at the Royal Albert Hall in October

1999, one pretty blonde 'model' and bit-part actress whose real name is Sandra, and who is endowed with rather more ambition than talent, made a huge play for him. She adjusted her minuscule dress to reveal an alarming amount of flesh and waited for Jools to leave Jamie's side. She was patient, and she had to be, because the couple remained close for most of the evening. But when Jools was forced to answer the call of nature, Sandra knew it was her chance to pounce.

She undulated across to Jamie and got as close as she could and then started whispering some lively suggestions about how they might spend the next few minutes. She was direct and demanding and she made it colourfully clear that only he could satisfy her every need. Jamie's expression hardly changed throughout the X-certificate suggestions and when Sandra paused for breath he smiled gently at her and said, 'You must be joking, darling,' before moving away.

'He is just not interested in other women,' said a friend. 'He gets loads of offers. Some of them even more blatant than Sandra's, if that is possible to imagine, and they are all politely rejected. I think he is more embarrassed than anything. He reckons it is a bit demeaning to the women and just a by-product of being on television. He said to me that he never had women coming up and wanting to sleep with him before he was on television. So he knows it is just the screen image they fancy, not him. To Jamie, it is about as bizarre as the lady old-age pensioners who reach out to grab his bottom when he is signing their copy of his book for them.'

He might appear to be the ultimate party animal with that flashing quick wit and bulging bank balance, but Jamie Oliver refuses to be slotted into predictable categories. Some passing friends tell him he should be out on the town with every available beautiful woman, but they don't stay friends very long. Jamie loves Jools and his real friends understand and respect that. So, in putting his master plan for marriage into action, what really motivated the young millionaire was a desire to give his stunning young bride the most amazing day of her life.

'Jamie knows he will only ever get married once, so he was absolutely determined to get it right,' said a friend, who went to the ceremony. 'He might seem all larky and Jack-the-lad and he knows that image goes down brilliantly on television. But there is a sensitive, thoughtful side to him as well, which viewers don't ever get to see.

'He hates cruelty and injustice of any sort. He is by no means a political animal. Although he was happy to cook for Tony Blair, he would certainly think twice about campaigning for him. Jamie's beliefs are really more to do with a slightly old-fashioned concept of fairness. He does not understand why in a country as rich as Britain some people live lives of grinding poverty half-way up tower blocks that they are afraid to come out of for fear of getting mugged. But cooking is his chosen way of making everyone's life that much more enjoyable and he concentrates on that rather than getting too distracted by politics.

'On a strictly personal level, he has a very traditional attitude to life and, of course, one of the reasons he wants to get married now is because he and Jools very much want to have children before too much longer.'

As the year 2000 opened, Jamie was in his element. His television series was going from success to success with foreign sales swiftly following British acclaim. *The Naked Chef* was screened in a dozen countries, including Italy, which delighted the star. Planning his own marriage seemed to be the last piece in the jigsaw to make his life complete.

Jamie Oliver is a firm believer in the institution of marriage. He realises that he has been fortunate enough to grow up with a mother and father who have a very happy and fulfilling marriage and he has seen at first hand what a deeply enriching foundation for life that can provide. At the start of a new century, Jamie and Jools felt that the time was right for them.

But the big wedding of the Essex year almost went wrong even before it began, because Jamie's mother mistakenly booked the wrong church on the wrong date! Jamie said, 'She was so excited she rushed out and booked one of the churches in Clavering. Luckily we realised in time.'

The couple wanted to marry in nearby Rickling where his parents live, rather than in Clavering, site of The Cricketers, the pub where Jamie diced his first carrots under his father's careful tuition.

The couple laughed off the blunder but Jamie's mum was a little embarrassed. The whole family was so determined to make the day special she simply wanted to book the church as soon as possible. But the right church was fortunately still available and it was quickly reserved.

'We were not able to arrange anything before now because last year we were just too busy,' said Jamie. 'And before that we just couldn't afford it. We were always too skint.

'I love Jools very much and marriage means a great deal to me. It is a very special thing and we are both ready to take our vows. Jools and I both come from good solid families, who believe in marriage, and it makes perfect sense to take the decision now. We have been going out for seven years so I think we are certain.'

In fact, Jamie has proposed to Jools many times in their relationship. Some three years earlier he popped the question when she was working as a waitress at a restaurant called Maxwell's in London's Hampstead. She accepted straight away but the couple were so hard up they both knew they would have to wait. Jamie says he had been looking forward to marrying Jools for years and 'I just can't wait to see her walk down the aisle in a wedding dress and veil.'

Jamie and Jools also shared the conviction that children would benefit from being born to parents who were happily living in wedlock. 'I think it is fairer to bring up kids if you are married,' said Jamie. 'I would like to start on a family as soon as possible and I know Jools is keen to get cracking. I think we will make good parents. I would love a little four-year-old kid right now, but Jools has not wanted to have a child before now. Maybe now is the time and I am looking forward to it.'

Preparations were well under way long before the big day. Jamie had already made his wedding cake which was sitting in a cupboard under the stairs being fed regular slurps of alcohol which were to make it even more interesting. But with a few months to go before the big day, the menu had still to be finalised in detail. Jamie mused, 'We'll probably have a really fabulous antipasti, whatever is in season, with really good olive oil and some bread. I know I will probably get up at five or six and make a load of bread for 150. The main course will be roasted fish. I have decided to be spontaneous and have told my dad that as far as the food is concerned I am going to go to the market the day before to see what looks really good and fresh. It is driving him up the wall. I can't tell you exactly what it is going to be but it will be something simple and will comprise the best quality ingredients money can buy. I am getting a couple of my boys down from London to oversee the preparation but generally it will be cooked by the team from my dad's pub The Cricketers.

'Dad has already planted these really special ratte pataters, so we'll have those boiled with a little butter maybe and some dill from the garden and rocket, big bowls of salad, not wanky stuff.'

Jamie enthused, 'It's going to be a wild night. We're getting married at our local church in the village of Rickling and from there we'll walk back to the house, where we're putting up a big marquee, eating ourselves stupid and the dancing all night. I am really hoping that the Chemical Brothers will be able to come to do some DJ'ing. I have done a deal with Tom. I have promised to cook at his wedding and in return he has promised to DJ at mine.

'I have wanted to get married to Jools for years. She is the sexiest, coolest person I know and the only reason we didn't get married years ago was that we couldn't afford it.'

One of the most difficult problems for the wedding organisers was sorting out the guest list. Jamie admitted that he had had to be 'a bit controversial' with relatives and had ruled out anyone they hadn't seen for five years or longer. And they had decided not to invite all of their parents' friends. It would be mostly Jamie and Jools's friends who kept the party going long into the night. To make matters even more complicated, Jamie said, 'Another problem is that only half of the guests are coming to eat. A hundred are arriving later for the party and we have already got to get rid of 30 people from the dinner list.'

Viewers of *The Naked Chef* did get to see Jamie preparing a meal with the in-laws as they planned the big wedding. But he firmly drew the line at allowing anyone in to film their June nuptials. Jamie says, 'This new TV series does show some really personal stuff. But we've got to stop at some point. And we have turned down all the magazine offers to come and photograph us. There's no way we are selling the wedding in any way. We want it to be laid back and chilled and about us and our family and friends.'

Jamie was stunned by the size of the offers he received from assorted glossy magazines wanting exclusive rights to film the happy day. 'They have offered us loads of cash,' said Jamie. 'Around £250,000. It is an immense amount, obscene money, and I'll admit we find it tempting to take it. We probably can't really afford to turn it down, but we are going to say "No" on a moral basis, because it's tacky and naff.'

In fact, Jamie could have made much more than that, but once he had made his mind up he was not going to change it for even the most ludicrous offer.

Jamie sympathised with his friends Zoë Ball and Fatboy Slim because a magazine had managed to get hold of various photos of their wedding from one of the guests and had printed them with the sarcastic note that 'the wedding would have been so much better if we'd done it'.

'That was so ridiculous,' said Jamie.

'It's funny, Jamie was really tough about this point,' said a friend. 'He is so accommodating with the press normally that I was surprised. And a quarter of a million pounds is an awful lot of cash to turn down. But he can afford it and he wanted the day to be absolutely perfect. He didn't want to be beholden to anyone to have to pose up for "just one more, please" for any greasy photographer. And more than that, he told me later, after he'd had a drink or two, that the wedding was so special to him that he couldn't bear the thought of anyone "owning" it. He said he knew he was only ever going to get married once and he knew he would always regret it if he sold the rights to what should be a wonderful personal family occasion to any magazine.'

Jamie even kept his stag night under control, although a photo of a pal mooning did creep into the tabloids. The Naked Chef certainly approved. Jamie says, 'Moonies really make me laugh. It doesn't matter how grumpy or sad I am feeling, if someone pulls a moonie, it make me laugh. Moonies make the world go round.'

Jamie and friends enjoyed a drink or two on a night out in Brighton in the Mash Tun pub and assorted other hostelries. Jamie escaped pretty lightly in the fun stakes just before he got married. His chums did attempt to clingfilm him to a lamppost for a wheeze but he escaped just in time and legged it.

On the big day, Jamie got up at the crack of dawn to bake bread for his own wedding. 'We made up a new bread for the wedding,' he said enthusiastically. 'We rolled it out flat and rubbed it with three different flavours. We had the black of the olives, the green of smashed basil and the red of cherry tomatoes. We had wonderful salamis and the most amazing cheese. And I did just classic things that I have done over the past five years, like fresh cannellini beans braised slowly and then drizzled with good olive oil in a little herb vinegar and lots of parsley. And baby artichokes with boiled lemons, honey, roasted almonds and smashed thyme. It was all in bowls, and when I was sitting on the top table, I looked round the marquee. People were pouring stuff, ripping bread, passing olive oil, and every table was like that which was just how I wanted it to be.'

Jamie insisted on paying for the £50,000 wedding in full himself. For Jamie, it was like a present from him and Jools to both of their families. He is so grateful for the upbringing his parents gave him that he wanted to give them the sort of day he knew they would both really love. He and Jools organised everything like a military operation.

Jools arrived 15 minutes late from her home in nearby Saffron Walden in a 1951 Cadillac, followed by the bridesmaids – her sisters Lisa and Nathalie and best friend Nicola Duguid – in a pale green 1955 Buick Roadmaster that had been hired specially for the day.

Jamie waited nervously for his bride to arrive and confided to well-wishers, 'This is more nerve-racking than cooking for Tony Blair.'

The beautiful bridesmaids escorted Jools up the aisle. Best man was Jamie's best friend and fellow chef Ben O'Donoghue. Jamie walked the 200 yards from the family home to the church and later surprised his bride by organising a serenade from an Elvis Presley impersonator who sang 'I Can't Help Falling in Love with You' after the traditional service at the thirteenth-century All Saint's Church. Even the vicar, Reverend Anthony Lindsay, joined in the song. Wedding guest Doreen Winterflood said, 'It was the most laid-back wedding I have ever been to.'

And Juliette's proud mother Felicity said, 'It was lovely, so relaxing. The service was very Jamie and Juliette.'

The only embarrassment for Jamie was when his middle name of Trevor was read out by the vicar. His friends in the congregation were distinctly heard to giggle. 'I had managed to keep it secret all my life until my wedding,' winced Jamie afterwards.

Jools wore a strapless white dress designed by Neil Cunningham with ankle-strapped white stiletto shoes designed by Jimmy Choo. Jamie was dressed in a sky-blue corduroy suit by Paul Smith – who was among the wedding guests – and a pink open-necked shirt, purple socks and grey snakeskin loafers.

Jools walked up the aisle on the arm of Jamie's father and afterwards the groom happily admitted that his heart missed a beat when he saw his breathtaking bride. A friend who was at the wedding said, 'After everything that has happened to him in the last few years, it was still unbelievable the effect the wedding had on Jamie. He so wanted everything to be perfect. The food had to be superlative, of course, and it was, but Jamie was so concerned that everything else ran smoothly as well. And loads of old friends from school were there. They are very important to Jamie. He likes a bit of the high life, of course, but he's often said that he'd rather have a meal and a drink with old friends than a slap-up banquet with Posh and Becks or anyone famous.'

'Fame is crap, mate,' he once said with typical economy. 'The press people are mainly fine but, after a while, the endless intrusion does get in the way of your life. You have to carve out some pieces that nobody gets near, where you can just be yourself and not worry about whether somebody is going to ask just one more question or want to take one more blasted photograph.'

As Jamie and Jools came out of the church after the ceremony, Jamie gave a thumbs-up sign to his waiting fans and admirers outside and joked, 'The service was beautiful. I feel good. We had good fun. I'm bloody happy. We're off for a kebab.'

Jamie was delighted to hit exactly the right fashion note. He said, 'Jools had been completely secretive about the dress, so I thought I'd better look a bit sharp and had my suit made up by Paul Smith. I've never had one made before. The brief was 60s pimp – sky-blue corduroy, mate, with turn-back cuffs, which sounds weird but looks absolutely pukka. No tie. Very *Quadrophenia*,' he added in a reference to the cult '60s film about Mods.

And on top of the wedding plans, Jamie had arranged a three-week honeymoon to Italy which took some organising as they were also deeply involved in buying their first proper flat together at the time. 'It was just the time that everything came together for me,' said Jamie. 'I don't mind spending money on Jools and my family. That's why I work so hard. I am so lucky to have enjoyed this success but what is the point of leaving money in the bank? I believe it is here to be enjoyed while you're young.'

'I am really looking forward to going to Italy,' said Jamie. 'I can't wait. I'm going to Italy for three weeks for a bit of beef jerky, some good tucker, some fresh air, bit of sunshine, and to put a bun in the oven. Know what I mean! I have never had a two-week holiday in my life before and now we are having three weeks. It is going to be incredible, although I probably won't know what to do with myself after ten days.'

The lease on the two-bedroom flat the couple had been sharing in West London had just run out and Jamie and Jools had just bought a new house in the same area. 'It is a shame in a way, we have just got the flat looking nice,' says Jamie. 'When we first moved in it was a dump and the flat downstairs was a doss house. It was full of tramps and it really used to stink. But luckily they have moved out and we have done it up nicely with loads of decent furniture and appliances. It is a shame to move on but the new place is going to be brilliant, even though it does need loads of work. It is a little cottage and we are both very excited with it.'

When Jamie married Juliette Norton, his school sweetheart, it was, according to several survivors, a vintage Essex bash with 140 guests, including half the county's pub trade, and The Chemical Brothers, helicoptered in from the Glastonbury pop festival at the groom's expense.

The food was unsurprisingly delicious by all accounts. The menu began with an appetising Bresaola made from organic topsides of beef and salami with artichokes with lemon and almonds, smashed-up thyme and honey, served with marinated olives, plates of plum tomatoes, grilled baby zucchini, red peppers and aubergine, with ripped basil and olive oil. The main course was wild salmon stuffed with herbs, onion and lemon, basted with olive oil and juices while cooking and served with a green salad and ratte potatoes tossed in butter and fennel tops.

For dessert, Jamie dished up organic strawberries and raspberries picked from the farm down the road the day before the wedding 'so they feel like they're still warm from the sun and have that stunning just-pulled-up flavour', served with beaten mascapone cream with vanilla and sugar.

When they married, Jools's father was thoughtfully remembered by an apple at every place setting on the tables at the reception because he had always called his beloved daughter the 'apple of my eye'. Jamie's grandfather Ted had also sadly died of a stroke and, as a mark of respect and love for both men, Jamie and Jools decided to use their big day to help stroke sufferers. Instead of wedding presents, guests were asked to give donations to the Stroke Association.

Jools explained, 'We both feel very strongly that young people should be more aware of the devastating effects a stroke can have. We have come to realise just how little is known about strokes, especially by people of our age. It is not seen as a trendy illness like breast cancer, but we believe it deserves just as much attention.'

The couple were pleased to forego wedding gifts to make their heartfelt point. 'We already have enough pots and pans for the kitchen,' said Jools.

The couple have spent much time and effort supporting stroke appeals ever since and Jamie was very proud to be asked to open the new stroke unit at Addenbrookes Hospital in Cambridge last year. He said at the time, 'Not a lot of people know how frustrating it is to have a stroke and how disruptive it is for the family. It is very underrated compared with things like cancer or AIDS, but now I am in a position where I can make a difference and help to make other people aware of what it is like.'

It was a day of high emotion and even Jamie's father was in tears. 'My dad is hard in business but underneath he is soppy,' says Jamie. 'Jools has taken him on as if he was her own father, which is exactly what I wanted. My dad is touched that she has embraced him so much. I think she needs it as well. She has missed a father figure.'

The wedding reception was held in a marquee in Jamie's parents' garden. After the fabulous food, Jamie's father made a speech. 'He spoke about Maurice and of the time he first really met him which was at Jools's sister's wedding,' said Jamie. 'Dad said that when everyone was running around and kind of ignoring Maurice, he saw me kneel down and joke with him and be quite touchy-feely. He said that sometimes a son can teach a father something and he wished he could have been more like that with Maurice. My dad's lips were quivering and the whole room was in tears. I was just staring at my feet as I always do when I'm feeling something deeply. I find it hard to cry.

'But then Dad completely changed. We had gone through the emotional bit with people crying and suddenly he said, "Now I am going to take the piss out of Jamie." And two of my mates carried in this 6ft door. My dad had saved my toy cupboard door from when I was a kid. That was when we moved from living in the pub to our own house. It was covered in pictures of naked women. It was the classic Essex boy adolescence and I must say I haven't changed all that much. I'm still pathetic. There were all the pictures of breasts stuck together that looked like rolling hills. Dad said, "When I asked Jamie what they were he said, 'It's wonderful countryside, Dad.'" Everybody was laughing at my expense and Dad went on to describe in detail everything on that door.

'Afterwards, I got up to thank Jools and Mum and Dad. I thanked everybody in the room, really, because we only invited people who were special to me and Jools.'

The day finished with a lively disco and a fireworks display at 12.30am. 'Like most people, we had our hefty arguments about the whole wedding vibe,' said Jamie. 'I started saying, "Whatever you like, darling," and craving a quiet life. For dancing we had a list of tacky romantic tunes to keep Jools happy, but if it had been down to me it would have been The Prodigy and stuff. But, like I say, it was, "Whatever you like, darling."'

They enjoyed a blissful honeymoon together in Italy but the success of *The Naked Chef* is such that it is almost impossible for Jamie to escape completely. The honeymoon was briefly interrupted at one point when even in a remote and tiny Italian village a fan spotted the Naked Chef and ran up waving a book to be autographed.

Chapter Seven

The Beat Goes On

Jamie Oliver entered the world at a time when it's safe to say that the British nation was displaying a taste in popular music which could be described at best as both eclectic and eccentric. How else could a mediocre fun group like Mud vie for the number one spot in the pop charts with Nashville's queen of country music Tammy Wynette and two of BBC TV's most popular comedy stars of the time, Windsor Davies and Don Estelle?

Mercifully for the newborn Jamie, who was of course destined to become a fanatical musician and an enthusiastic rock drummer, Mud's 'Oh Boy', Tammy's song of female devotion 'Stand by Your

Man', and 'Whispering Grass' by the two actors from the BBC sit-com *It Ain't Half Hot Mum*, would not have registered with such infant ears back in May 1975.

But as Jamie began growing up, it soon became clear that he did have a natural ear for music. The first record which he ever remembers making a major impact upon him was 'Everybody Wants to Rule the World' by Tears for Fears.

'I was about nine and at primary school,' he recalls, 'and I was at a youth hostel at Bradwell in Essex right near the power station. Essex is very large and from where I come from Bradwell was a long way away. The record was a hit at a point when you started fancying girls and I remember we had a snooker table and a juke box and this tune "Everybody Wants to Rule the World" kept coming on. Every time I hear it, it brings back kinda soppy memories and I always try and sing to it – and get it wrong.'

Significantly, 'Everybody Wants to Rule the World', which reached number two in the charts in March 1985, had a distinctive and unusual drum beat which caught Jamie's ear and sowed an early seed in his musical development.

'Everybody Wants to Rule the World' was, by all accounts, a very different kind of record from the music he was used to hearing at home and in the car when Jamie's mum was driving him to and from school. 'I didn't really listen to a lot of music at home when I was growing up,' he says. 'But what I did listen to was dreadful. My parents had terrible taste. My mum used to get all the ballads. My mum is actually a bit of a boy racer and her car was always a bit of a state, you know, Marks and Spencer's sarnies everywhere and milkshakes, and she'd put ballads on so loud and I'd be sitting there in the car getting taken to school going, "Oh no!" to someone singing, "This is the greatest love of all".'

Around the time Jamie's ears were first beginning to pick up on the popular sounds of the day, he struck up a friendship with a new arrival at his primary school in Clavering who was to have a lasting impression upon him in the music sphere. His name was Leigh Haggerwood, a Hertfordshire-born boy whose family had moved to Clavering when Leigh was eight.

Jamie remembers first setting eyes on Leigh turning up at his school wearing a purple bodywarmer and, as can often happen to the new boy at school, Leigh was largely ignored by the other lads and eyed with some suspicion. He was sitting at his desk feeling thoroughly neglected and not a little sorry for himself when the classroom door swung open and in walked Jamie. Noting Leigh's isolation while other boys were chattering away in groups, Jamie felt sorry for the newcomer and went over and introduced himself in a cheery, matey way and explained that he lived at the local pub. 'We clicked straight away,' Leigh recalls. 'I invited him round to my house the following weekend and he was just like a little ray of light, even back then.'

It was the start of a terrific and long-lasting friendship that would eventually see the two boyhood pals grow up to form the core members of a pop group they were to call Scarlet Division. But that was some years away. On that cold winter's day when they first met at primary school, there was little hint that they would team up musically on a serious basis. Both took up playing keyboards at an early age but, as befits boys of eight, they were more into which tree they would climb next rather than learning the fingering for the next chord.

Over the next three years, Jamie and Leigh became firm pals, often to be found at each other's homes and Jamie was genuinely upset when Leigh told him one day that he would be leaving the village and moving away with his family to Devon.

At first, Leigh kept in contact by sending the occasional postcard, but Jamie rarely wrote back.

He was ashamed of his spelling and hated his own handwriting. It was inevitable that, as the months went by, they more or less lost touch and Jamie found other friends to play with.

But when Jamie was 12 and had moved on to Newport Free Grammar School, he was racing down the stairs at the start of a new term when he saw a familiar face. It was Leigh, who went on to explain to Jamie that he had just moved back to Essex. The two lads were pleased to see each other, but it was something of an awkward reunion as they stopped to talk on the stairs. Jamie was a bit embarrassed that he had failed to keep up much of a correspondence with Leigh during his years in Devon. Also, they had both changed and grown up a great deal. The last time they had seen each other they were both little boys in short trousers. Time had moved on, and over the next few months they did not see much of each other as Jamie, being older than Leigh, was a year above him.

Then one day the two boys got talking music again and Leigh casually mentioned his fervently held ambition, that he was trying to get a band together. He was surprised and delighted to learn that Jamie had moved on to playing the drums rather than keyboards and with great enthusiasm they set about forming a group. It was a catalyst for re-kindling the great friendship they had once shared.

By now Jamie's parents had moved out of The Cricketers into a home of their own, a cottage not exactly purpose-built for a teenager with energy to burn beating a drum kit. But they were keen to encourage Jamie's enthusiasm for music and his desire to play the drums and, to accommodate Jamie's burgeoning interest and his avowed intention of getting a group together with Leigh, a shed was built in the garden where the sound of his bass drum, the sizzle, and the high hat could reverberate without shaking the cottage to its foundations.

The shed quickly became known as Scarlet House and Scarlet Division seemed to be a good name for Jamie's and Leigh's embryonic band. There the two boys practised as often as they could, promising themselves that one day they'd be on *Top of the Pops* like some of the bands they went off to see in action at the Cambridge Corn Exchange.

Their band only really started to take shape with the arrival of dark-haired Louise Brannan as lead singer. Louise, from Ilkeston, Derbyshire, was not only talented vocally but she was beautiful, too. By the time she was summoned for an audition by Jamie and Leigh, Louise had already paid some musical dues singing in pubs accompanying herself on guitar.

Ironically, in view of Jamie's culinary talents, Louise had taken a catering course at Buxton College and had become a qualified chef. 'But I'm not in Jamie's league,' she says. 'He's a brilliant cook. I've always been a singer and just done the odd cooking job to keep my head above water – mostly things like cooking for old people's homes.'

Louise had arrived in Essex to take up a catering job at a college and then met Jamie and Leigh after moving to another job at Stansted Airport. 'I was auditioned for the band in the shed they called the Scarlet House,' she remembers. 'Hence the name of the band. Jamie has told interviewers some cock-and-bull stories about the name being inspired by seeing the sunset between two trees, but it really came from the shed.'

With Leigh displaying a flair for song composition, things started looking bright for Scarlet Division. But once Jamie went off to catering college and began pursuing his career in cooking, Scarlet Division inevitably took second place in his life.

'We played together for a while,' says Louise, 'but then Leigh and I did our own thing. We travelled all over doing covers.'

It was while Leigh and Louise were gigging around the world together that they gained their first experience of TV, long before Jamie, appearing on Canadian TV in a live concert for Amnesty International and later on a programme in Beirut.

This time, the absences did not prevent Leigh and Jamie keeping in touch with each other and they regularly swapped stories of how their respective lives were progressing, always swearing that one day they'd get Scarlet Division back together.

By the time Jamie was working at The River Café, Leigh and Louise had moved to London and once again had resumed their close friendship with Jamie. 'When we decided to start up the band again, Jamie wanted in,' says Louise.

But to flesh out the Scarlet Division sound, they decided they needed to get serious. It was necessary to recruit a guitarist and a bass player, positions which were eventually filled by Andy Baker and James Bejon. With the addition of these two, Scarlet Division reached a much higher level musically because Baker and Bejon were two serious musicians with track records to prove it.

Bejon's musical credentials included classical training in piano and clarinet. After taking a Maths degree at Warwick University, he moved to London where he played in various bands and was good enough to be hired for session work. Baker had first started playing guitar at the age of eight and

Santana and Fleetwood Mac were among his earliest musical influences.

Andy had an elder brother, Terry, who would teach him chords and songs and Terry's eventual progression to playing with Carmel and Pulp only persuaded Andy to practise his guitar even harder in order to become proficient in varying styles of guitar playing. He formed his first band at 14 and, on leaving school, he played with a group called The Wicked Things before moving to London to join The Blow Monkeys.

Jamie's sudden TV success after being spotted in the documentary for The River Café might have spelled the end of Scarlet Division. But it says much for the friendship of the band members, and for the patience of Leigh and Louise especially, that they were prepared to bide their time and wait to link up with Jamie as Scarlet Division when time and opportunity allowed. Even when *The Naked Chef* suddenly turned Jamie into one of the most in-demand TV newcomers, Jamie repaid their faith in him and their patience by jumping on his scooter to ride over to the east end of London to attend rehearsals. It was his proud boast that, despite all his TV commitments, he never missed one.

Scarlet Division's willingness to put up with the meteoric rise to fame of their drummer in a totally different field was also recognised when Jamie got the band together and came up with the idea of having the new line-up filmed for the programme doing their first gig at The Falcon in Camden, North London.

Accordingly, in May 1999, *The Naked Chef* show featured Jamie cooking a Thai curry for the band to eat when they returned from the gig. There had been talk of Scarlet Division writing a theme tune for *The Naked Chef*, but when that idea failed to materialise, this was at least a brief showcase for the band.

It wasn't long before Jamie and Scarlet Division were attracting interest from record companies. Of course, by now, they understandably saw Jamie as a highly marketable prospect, although he himself was anxious not to steal the lion's share of Scarlet Division's limelight. Happily for all concerned, there was one record company who were prepared to come up with a deal to keep everyone happy.

Jamie had barely made it through the baggage reclaim on his return from his Italian honeymoon with Jools when it was announced that he and his band Scarlet Division had been signed up by the music giant Sony in a two-album deal believed to be worth more than £100,000.

First up would be *Jamie Oliver's Cookin'*, a

compilation CD of the songs Jamie liked to listen to while working his culinary magic. It would be followed by a record by Scarlet Division.

'Jamie's always loved music,' said the band's manager Alan Seisert. 'It's just there's never been any money in it.'

Jamie, who describes Scarlet Division's sound as 'somewhere between Texas, The Pretenders and modern techno' insists that the record deal had been earned by the band on merit and had nothing to do with his fame as a TV chef. 'My name has never been mentioned on any promotion for the band,' he said. 'The *NME* (*New Musical Express*) even gave us a favourable write-up.'

When Jamie had first been pitched the notion of an album of music to cook by, he quickly dismissed it. But within a few weeks, he had completely changed his mind. 'I thought it was a load of rubbish when they first came to me with the idea,' he said. 'But I was at home about a month later cooking with music on and I thought how much music is actually an integral part of my *Naked Chef* programme. I realised it was actually a very good idea.'

Typically, Jamie threw himself into the project once he'd made up his mind to go ahead with it. 'I said I'd only do it if I could be involved with the design so I got the art work done by a friend and used a food photographer for the jacket.'

The outcome was an eclectic mix of tracks chosen from Jamie's own record collection. It included 'Begging You' by The Stone Roses; Finlay Quaye's 'Even After All'; 'Dancing In The Moonlight' by Toploader; 'Motorcycle Emptiness' by the Manic Street Preachers; and '6 Underground' by Sneaker Pimps. Jamie commented, 'Putting the album together was a real trip down memory lane,' he said. 'Some of the people on the record I used to worship. My generation has had some cracking music to listen to over the years and if these tracks give people half as much pleasure as they've given me, then that's me sorted.'

In a clever piece of marketing, the last track on the album was 'Sundial' by Scarlet Division which would also be issued as the band's début single. In the sleeve notes, Jamie revealed that Sundial had been written by Leigh Haggerwood at a time of huge frustration for him when everyone was telling him to give up music and get a proper job. Cheekily, Jamie added in his notes on Scarlet Division. 'Fantastic drummer who's also an excellent cook.' He also thanked his parents for allowing him to play so much of his music at home.

Jamie and the rest of Scarlet Division were

thrilled to be cutting a record and Jamie was especially thrilled just to be in a proper recording studio. Ironically, Toploader just happened to be recording in the same studios at the same time and Jamie had chosen their 'Dancing in the Moonlight' for one of his TV shows. He'd liked the song from the moment he'd first heard it. While being shown around the Sony studios, Jamie was taken in to see a group rehearsing and it was only later he was told that they were Toploader. He hadn't recognised them. 'I just said, "How's it going, boys?" It was only a week later I realised who they were. The sad thing is I wanted to say, "Nice one." They're a very cool band, good boys. Lead singer with a fantastic voice, true voice, freaky haircut, real salt-of-the-earth boys.'

Jamie was able to express his respect for Toploader when he was invited to be a special guest on the MTV show *Ten of the Best* to be interviewed by Clare Grogan about his favourite songs. Inevitably, his choice corresponded for the most part with the songs he had chosen for *Jamie Oliver's Cookin'* CD, but it did give a revealing insight into his musical tastes.

'I can safely say I like all music at the right time and place,' he explained. 'I'm not a big rave boy, but if there's the atmosphere, the lights, then rave's cool. I wouldn't say I'm a classical boy, but on a chilled-out day a bit of half-decent classical is fine. I must say, I'm a bit of an indy, kinda like rock-band boy. But I'm really open to everything. But moods do say what you feel like. I dance around the house. I wouldn't dance in front of the missus because I'm too bad. I do do it, but I don't want to advertise my dancing.'

Running through his list of favourites, Jamie likes his music with soul. Like frozen ready meals, disposable pop leaves him cold. Of Jamiroquai's Jay Kay he declared, 'He's an extraordinary chap, the only chap who can dance upside down and still hit Stevie Wonder notes. In these days of backing tapes and the singers getting the old faders pushed up and not actually singing live, big respect going out to Jay Kay of Jamiroquai and to one of his original tracks, "Blow Your Mind", which I think is a bit of a classic. It was a big hit when I was 17 in the early days of Essex and had just passed my driving test in my Fiesta which was worth £1,000 and the stereo was worth £2,000. I was not one of those boys who drove round the town with the volume full up but this is one of those tunes that if I was, I would.'

The Happy Mondays, and particularly their song 'Loose Fit', Jamie revealed, were very much part of his early teenage life. 'England, indy, white label time. The Happy Mondays, fantastic band, brilliant drummer with a singer kinda outrageous but couldn't sing to save his life. Respect going to him because if you can't sing and you've got four people who can sing, I think that deserves just as much respect. It was the time of tie-dye tops, raving when you weren't really old enough to rave and very, very baggy flares, possibly frayed at the bottom.'

Jamie also picked out 'There She Goes' by The La's. 'Fantastic band,' he said, 'but bit of a disappointment, was said to be the next kinda Beatles. Everyone believed at the time they came out that they could be.

'A British band I've got a lot of respect for, because they've been there for 12 years, is The Charlatans and their "My Beautiful Friend". I saw them at Reading when they did their first gig for four years and they were fantastic. And they came back with a massive album. I've seen them about four times. The drummer gets right into it, sweats a bit and looks as ugly as I do when I drum. Bit of dribbling every now and then.

'Fatboy Slim, I think he's the king of re-invention, along with Madonna and other genius people in our world. I think he's so clever. I've met him many times and he's a very nice guy. I wouldn't say I know him very well. He is a true genius but plays it down.'

Other Jamie favourites included The Style Council, Cast and Duran Duran, of whom he said, 'I was never really into them in their early days because I was too young. But I always respect people who write their own stuff and are a true band and no matter how old they get, they beat that five-year shelf-life and kept going.

'The Stone Roses are also a fruity little English Manchester band. After that classic little album with the lemon on it, they didn't do anything for so long. Then they came out with an EP with the song "Fool's Gold" on it. It was a good tune and good to have them back after four years.

'Any of these bands I've listed I'd be happy to be a drummer in, not one of those composed we-don't-actually-sing-but-look-pretty, kind of thing, but a proper band.'

Jamie and the other members of Scarlet Division had high hopes for their début single 'Sundial' when it was released in October of 2000. An upbeat number with some great vocal gymnastics by Louise and driven along by Jamie's backbeat, 'Sundial' sold well enough to register just above the Top 40 with the help of a jacket which featured a colour photo of Jamie in a van driving the band with Louise and Leigh beside him in the front seat. A little round sticker on the record case announced 'With Jamie Oliver on drums.'

Around the time of the record's release, Jamie had his musical abilities laid bare when Scarlet Division performed to a global audience via a Radio 1 webcast. Jamie appeared on Zoë Ball's radio show and agreed to perform at the station's live gig in Manchester when she suddenly told him, 'I've got you a gig at Radio 1 Live in Manchester this Sunday afternoon. It's not big time, just 10,000 people alongside the likes of James, Melanie C, Supergrass and All Saints.'

Then she added, tongue in cheek, 'But I promise you if you're no good we will all leg it. So get to rehearsing, darling.' Jamie, whose biggest crowd with Scarlet Division to date had been 300, wasn't fazed however.

'Great!' he said. 'Then I can say I've supported them all. I'm gonna live it large!'

The memory of that gig in Heaton Park is one which will always stay with Jamie. 'It was 10,000 people, the first proper gig we ever did, we were first on. One of the last bands on was Supergrass, fantastic band, three boys, looked a bit scruffy and as handsome as you like and the sound those boys make. Three instruments, fat sound and not only a fat sound, they groove, make you feel good. The audience were going off and I was standing three metres away from the drummer. Fantastic.'

It would be easy for his critics to point the finger at Jamie and say he is a dilettante musician, a TV star who is cashing in on his fame to try and make it as a rock star. It's the same burden that other famous celebrities like Keanu Reeves, Bruce Willis and Russell Crowe all have to bear when they step up on stage as musicians.

But Jamie stoutly defends his position with Scarlet Division. 'We're true troupers,' he says. 'We've done the rounds, we've done all the venues in London. I've been in the band since I was 12, same three key members, but we've had about 37 guitarists. After 12 years we've had our chance.'

To promote 'Sundial', Jamie and the band made a video on the cheap begging favours wherever they could. It was filmed in a field in the heart of the countryside with the group performing on a makeshift stage. Into the field comes a farmer with a goat but instead of raising merry hell at the musical intrusion he starts to move in time to the music. Pretty soon a crowd gathers which gets bigger and bigger. When the number ends, there is just one desultory handclap from the crowd and a bleat of approval from the goat. Given its financial limitations, it was an effective video and somewhere in the crowd was Jools and Jamie's nan.

'We had a really small budget to do the video,' said Jamie, 'and we blagged so many favours and even me nan was in it giving it large with the old Zimmer.'

Jamie jokes a lot about his musical ambitions but when he plays he is deadly serious. He is not keen to wear his heart on his sleeve but he really believes in Scarlet Division and nothing would please him more than a hit record. In his heart, he always feels a shade guilty that perhaps his astonishing cooking success has somehow queered the pitch of the band and prevented them from being taken seriously as a musical unit. It never seems fair to Jamie that the band do get tagged with having The Naked Chef on drums rather than simply listened to for their music. But he is so close to the other members now that he hopes with time the band will be accepted on their own merits. 'I am not playing at it,' he says. 'I would love the band to get success. Even if it would pose a few problems for me and my overcrowded schedule.'

Chapter Eight

Home-made

Jamie and Jools marked the start of their marriage with a new home, a two-bedroom flat in London's Hampstead, which needed quite a lot of work doing to it. In spite of all the dust and mess, Jamie insisted on carrying Jools over the threshold, but they both vowed they would repeat the procedure once all the building work had been completed. Jamie enthused, 'We enjoyed the house-buying process. We were lucky and it seemed easy-peasy. We had a great solicitor who made everything really quick. And it was a laugh looking round places in London, although Jools did most of the leg-work because I was pretty busy. We both loved this place as soon as we saw it.'

But the stylish love-nest had one big disadvantage. It was absolutely tiny. 'We both knew it was much too small,' said Jamie. But the couple decided that just meant they would have to be really clever with their use of space. And expand upwards! They devised a way of putting on an extension upstairs which gave them a really big bedroom and space for a sun veranda right on top. With his busy schedule, Jamie found it very daunting when he fully realised what the building entailed. 'When we first got the keys I thought, God, I haven't got time to take this on. But then I decided we would just have to make time.'

The couple lived in a rented place while the work was carried out. Jamie was impatient. 'I can't wait until we can get our new home looking the business and then move in. I am really looking forward to the flooring going down and the windows going in because at the moment they are really horrible modern things. We are trying to keep in tune with the building which is more than 300 years old, so we are having original-style windows put in.'

Not surprisingly, the first room Jamie wanted to get straight was the kitchen. It was very small but he reckoned that with some clever planning it could be well equipped and good to work in. But definitely without the cameras. It was much too small to cope with Jamie's equipment so it had to be completely stripped out. 'No mucking about,' said Jamie.

The couple were busy choosing a suitably stylish work surface and a wood oven which Jamie specified for pizzas and roast lamb especially. They decided to expose the old fireplace and install a real-flame gas fire to give their new home some warmth, and plenty of glass to ensure it was bright. There were quite comprehensive changes by the time they had thought through all their plans, with the second bedroom turned into a bathroom and the old bathroom converted into a spare room-cum-office. Jamie had an ideal in his mind and he would not settle for second best. But he said Jools was rather more relaxed about developments: 'Jools just wants to get rid of the dodgy yellow shower curtain and she will be happy. And when it comes to colour, I will definitely leave it to the missus. Not that I haven't got a feminine side. I can get into pastels. We really want to get it done now. It doesn't matter if you're The Naked Chef or Bill Bloggs, you still have to make the decision to do it all in one hit or do it over ten years. We just want to get it done as quickly as possible, because when it is finished it will almost be like the proper start of our married life.

'Now I always feel really proud every time I say "My wife". It sends a little shiver down my spine. Inside I think, I'm married, and I am still surprised. It feels like a really responsible thing that I have done.'

Since Jamie arrived on television, he has noticed a real change in Jools. 'In the past three years she has become so strong. She shocks me sometimes. It is nothing to do with my influence. It is just that she has turned into a woman. If anyone criticises me it upsets her, because I'm part of her now.'

Ever since Jamie's unconventional show became a hit, even his loved ones have been recognised in the street. And it now takes him at least one-and-a-half hours to nip to the supermarket because everyone wants a look in his basket.

'I get so embarrassed because the missus buys so much rubbish like fish fingers,' he says. 'I try to make it look like that's her stuff and this is mine. Sometimes I do get very excited about everything that has happened and I talk about it. But my missus has her feet firmly on the ground and all it takes is one look from her and I know that it's time to shut up.'

Jamie and Jools both resent the amount of time his busy schedule forces them apart. Jamie says, 'I do feel guilty about Jools, but I leave her little notes when I leave her asleep. And I speak to her ten times a day on the phone to make sure she is all right. I tell her I love her when I get home. But wives always get upset, don't they, and she worries about me. I am trying to make Sundays sacred and then I won't feel guilty.

'The only thing Jools cares about is me, you see. She is a bit like a mother. She feels that unless she asks millions of questions when I get home she is not doing her duty. I used to dream about marrying her before I even went out with her.

'I never had women really interested in me before I was on telly. It makes me thank God I found Jools first, because otherwise I would be thinking, Am I attractive just because I have earned a few bob? Jools keeps my feet on the ground and my head out of the clouds. She knows me better than I know myself. She is not jealous of other women because she knows I would never be unfaithful. What she is jealous of is not my reliability or my commitment, it is my time.'

Jamie modestly insists that he does not get that much attention from the opposite sex and he is plainly embarrassed when it does arrive. But he is much more surprised to have become something of a gay icon. Jamie says, 'I do get quite a lot of fan letters and many are from blokes. I got one really sexy letter saying, "I want to do this to you, I think you are this, I think you are that ..." I read half of it and thought it would be really funny to wind up Jools with it. So I read it out to her but the joke backfired when I got to the end and found out it had been signed, "Love from Paul".'

But Jamie plays down the impact he has on female fans. Young – and sometimes not-so-young – Jamie Oliver groupies used to wait outside the doors of the posh River Café restaurant. And his mailbag is full of female invitations. 'Most of the letters are from teenage girls,' he said. 'They make me giggle. Some even say they love me and want to meet me for a coffee. I reckon I should frame them and put them on the wall. But cooking is great if you are trying to pull a bird. Food can be sexy. You have to go for something you can share, like a whole lobster or a roast dinner. Make sure you get the food all over your face and have a laugh.'

The one thing everyone shouts at him in the streets, mentions casually to him at smart dinner parties, or even whispers to him in the most exalted surroundings is when is he going to get his kit off. Even the Prime Minister's wife Cherie Blair wanted to know why he was fully dressed when he arrived at number 10 Downing Street.

But the answer to the most asked question in Jamie Oliver's life – 'Oi! Naked! Are you going to take your clothes off?' – is always the same.

'No,' says Jamie. 'Not ever in public. It simply is not going to happen. Not for all the money in the world. You wouldn't like what you saw, anyway.

'I know that people are going to keep asking the question so long as I am called the Naked Chef. But for the ten millionth time,' he says with smile, 'the name was supposed to be a reference to the food being stripped right down to the bare essentials. Not me. But everyone expects to see me prancing around the kitchen in nothing but an apron. I have hated the title from day one but it has been a great brand name.

'I have only just started and I am not going to sell out. I am not in this just for the money, but because I love cooking.'

He did once try cooking without clothes on, it is fabled, but after he burned a particularly sensitive part of his body he firmly decided against ever trying it again. Jamie says, 'My advice is always wear an apron. Cooking can be quite dangerous. You don't want to scald anything that might help you procreate this lovely planet that we live on. I would hate to be responsible for that.'

Inevitably there is a down side to the rise and

rise of Jamie Oliver. He finds there are those who are forever searching for flaws in the squeaky-clean lifestyle.

'Now I am busy 18 hours a day and six days a week,' says Jamie. 'I have had two good years so people are gagging to stitch me up but they can't because I don't do drugs, I don't have affairs and I don't do things that I don't believe in.'

Privately, he is saddened by the restrictions that fame places on himself and Jools. In some of his more reflective moments, he has observed to friends that they do not know how lucky they are to be able to take a walk in the park or to the shops in total anonymity. Being a famous household name and living in London means being permanently in the public eye. 'I can't complain because I wanted the shows to be popular,' says Jamie. 'But there are just some times when I would love to be able to switch it off for a day or so.'

Indeed, Jamie's idea of a good night out is to remove himself from the celebrity hype totally. He tries to finish work early, meet up with ten good friends, have a drink, go for some 'tucker', then go home with the missus and have a bit of what he colourfully describes as 'beef jerky'.

Jamie is fiercely anti-drugs. He says, 'I know it is not fashionable to say it, but you won't catch me in the toilets snorting cocaine or dropping Es. It scares me far too much for one thing. I just think it is going to make me feel really bad and do things that I am not really happy about. I don't even like getting really bevvied up to be honest.

'Alcohol is great stuff if you don't abuse it. Being brought up in a pub, I love getting tiddly but I don't do it very often, really. I have never been a piss artist but on a summer's day I love a cold lager or a chilled beer, or a vodka and tonic with a good squeeze of fresh lime.

'I like to be in control all the time. I am a funny boy. I am just kind of obsessive, really obsessive about creativity. But the demands on my time do get pretty ridiculous. I went out at seven o'clock in the morning yesterday and got back at four o'clock in the morning today.'

Jamie is a firm believer in hard work and determination to forge the direction of your own life. 'We were made in such a way that we can become anything we like. You either rise above things and set your own moral standards, your own fashions and styles, or you copy other people and spend your life being a sheep. If you want to see it, go to Southend and look at the kids – they all dress, look, smell and do their hair exactly the same as each other.'

Jamie believes that drugs do immense harm,

particularly to vulnerable young people. And he and Jools know that drugs pose one of the biggest potential dangers for any children they have together. Jamie says, 'I don't want to preach or tell anyone how to live their life, but I do really dislike the way drugs have become so firmly embedded in society. When you hear some of the stories of the lives wrecked by drug-taking it makes you kind of sad and angry at the same time. I just think what a terrible waste.'

Chapter Nine

Serving up Aces

Even after all of his success Jamie still finds it strange to see himself on television. He was never remotely nervous about filming *The Naked Chef* because it was recorded at his own house and he was doing something he passionately enjoys, cooking. But his own distinctly ordinary self popping up on TV screens, book covers and posters all over the place he still finds slightly strange to deal with. But in rare moments of self-doubt, he falls back on what he loves and knows best – cooking.

Jamie has lots of strong views on cooking but, at the end of the day, he frankly admits, 'I like to eat everything. It doesn't matter to me if it is not my style. It is all an education to me. When we go out to dinner, I always make sure I order last, so that I can order what everyone else has not ordered. If I am in the kitchen, I like to cook all the ingredients with great care. Instead of putting a lot of work into presentation, I put a lot of work into getting good ingredients and marinating. I believe in simple cooking and simple serving.'

He likes to cook big things where he can be left with plenty of leftovers to eat over the next week and says, 'I think it makes a lot of sense economically as well. When you cook a joint, it is great to eat some more of it in sandwiches the next day. Look how much ham costs in the shops. It is ridiculously expensive and it is usually a load of old rubbish. So if you buy a bigger joint and cook extra, you can have great sarnies for ages. It is the same with bread. I make it once every three weeks or so now and I make loads of it and stick it in the freezer. Even after home-made bread has been frozen and reheated, it tastes better than the stuff they sell in the shops. And I have really got a thing about flour, if that is not too boring.

'Then again, I would be lost without herbs. If I was only allowed to use one, I think it would have to be rosemary or basil, probably. But if there were no herbs in the world, I would give up cooking. Herbs can transform dishes. I think perhaps my all-time favourite vegetarian meal is an Italian dish called *rottollo*. You get a big sheet of pasta about as big as a broadsheet newspaper. Then you braise spinach, garlic, marjoram, butter, salt and pepper. Let it cool down then flake in ricotta, Parmesan or Pecorino and that is it. You fold it up like a roulade, wrap it in a cloth and cook it in a fish kettle. It is a really amazing taste. It is almost meaty because of the marjoram and the butter.

'There are loads of candidates but I think absolutely the very best meal I have ever had was in Italy, and this 70-year-old woman made gnocchi – little potato dumplings in a fantastic, spicy tomato sauce – with morels from the forest. Then we had a salad with celery with warm artichokes, Parmesan and sliced white truffles. She also made a sort of roast chicken thing as well, which was a blinder. It was an education.

'You have chefs with degrees and things, and here's a 70-year-old woman without any formal training at all who had made the best meal for eight of us. Italy is certainly one of my favourite countries and also probably Spain if they still have siestas. It's the best way to spend your day.

'Apparently, in the old days, back when we were

still gorillas, we used to have them anyway. I always feel tired at about one in the afternoon. I would love to have siestas in my life. But I also love to work very hard. And I do not see why I should be shy about being proud of what I do. Although I say so myself, I have never seen anyone put across how to cook focaccio bread as well as I did in my series. It is a thing of beauty.

'I have never once said in the past year that I am the best cook in England, because I am not. I just enjoy cooking. And I have been lucky enough to have had the chance to express myself on television. You have to do just one thing well and they think you are a star!'

Jamie believes his own advice with a passion. He insists that his cookbooks are different from all the rest because of the way he strips cooking down to its barest essentials. Even total culinary amateurs can tackle his recipes with confidence. Even his home-made pasta can be produced by a complete novice.

'I've got this mate called Damian. He is a huge Maori rugby player who had never cooked in his life. I gave him the instructions and first time off he was making fantastic sheets of pasta. If you used to muck around with Playdoh as a child, you are not going to have any trouble making pasta.'

Jamie believes all herbs have their virtues but he

loves myrtle which is often used to draw the flavours out of suckling pig. 'Myrtle is terrific,' he says. 'It's like stinging nettles – who would ever have thought it could taste so good? But once it is washed and plunged into boiling salted water it loses all its sting, holds its shape and has a texture and taste like spinach. It is delicious and unusual.

'Everybody thinks that organics is a fashionable thing, but I think it's really old-fashioned. Seventy years ago, everything was bloody organic. And the only reason it's expensive now is because you've got 90 per cent of the country knocking up normal clobber and using sprays. And don't for one moment think that chemicals are cheap. They cost a fortune. I've just come back from Australia and New Zealand, where they are very cold on organics. They know they've got good produce, but it's sprayed with all sorts of malarkey.'

He is less enthusiastic about GM (genetically modified) foods. 'If you've got a genius working on stuff and experimenting, I don't think there's anthing wrong with that. But it's not; it's every Tom, Dick and Harry that's got a test tube and a bloomin' lab.'

Jamie urges prospective cooks to 'be curious. If you want to cook something new and interesting, you are half-way there.' Jamie's favourite dishes are simple and rustic, 'like the food I cooked when I was working abroad. Not poncy French food but the simple dishes made with great ingredients. Why make something any more complicated than it needs to be? If I am making risotto, for example, I choose a couple of nice seasonal vegetables, a complementary herb and cook it up into a nice juicy, oozing risotto.'

Jamie's favourite cuisine is Mediterranean and he particularly loves the food of Spain and Italy. 'They use lots of flavours. I am also curious about fusion. If I could have my way, I would spend every day cooking and eating in a different country.

'The world's best cook is my mum. She is not the world's most technical cook perhaps, but she makes the best Sunday roasts and fabulous puddings. Her Spotted Dick and her syrup puddings make me go weak at the knees. My family upbringing really taught me the importance of food to bring people together. When I was growing up in a family in the pub business, everyone was very busy. But the pub closed between 3.30pm and 6.00pm. So it was very important that we all sat down together for dinner at five o'clock. And it was not just for the food. That was the time for the whole family to sit around the table and have a proper talk. Of course, sometimes there were arguments as well but that was just part of the fun. I loved the easy, relaxed way we used to eat. We had big platters of food that were passed round and round and there were cans of beer and jugs of drink. It was an occasion and we all respected that. One day when I have children of my own, I want Jools and I to be with our children how my parents were with me and my sister. But if Jools ever cooked we would end up talking about it and end up as boring people. One of the worst meals I ever had was when Juliette prepared a very dodgy sausage and mash. I threw up afterwards.'

Jamie is always very generous with his time and he is always happy to answer questions from fans. But his quickfire responses sometimes surprise the questioners. As he put it, 'Size counts when it comes to ovens with me. The more knobs it has, the better.' And asked if he had got any other talents, he replied, 'I am not a bad drummer. I am not a bad artist. I am not a bad lover, either!'

What wine do you choose to accompany your meals?

'To be honest, the best thing to do is drink something you enjoy and you know. If it is a big robust red wine, have steak. If it is a delicate white wine, have fish. Quite frankly, there are no rules, have what you like.'

Jamie always encourages young people interested in cooking to follow their enthusiasm. He advises them to 'read lots of cookbooks and magazines and find out what chef inspires you and then write to them and say how you love what they do and ask if you can work with them for a while. If you work hard, they might give you a job.

'If I have a night off cooking and go down to the local kebab shop, they always take the mickey out of me for not cooking something for myself.'

Jamie refuses to take his job too seriously. When one fan from Billericay asked if he ever tried to bring any Essex feelings into his dishes, he replied, 'Yeah. Sometimes I do it with no knickers on.'

But his tip on how to lose weight was eminently sensible. 'Stop buying butter, cream or cheese. Use extra virgin olive oil which is much better for you. Avoid red meat and cook lots of vegetables and use herbs. Healthy food doesn't have to be boring and with the use of herbs, spices, fish, seafood, white meat and veg you are laughing, especially if you can try baking things with minimal fat. If you fancy a munchy, have a bit of fruit. You can buy wheatless flour and stuff like that if you have wheat intolerance or anything like that and avoid pasta as it slows your metabolism down. You can get some great stuff now. Stick to Thai and Asian food, it's very healthy.'

Fortunately for Jamie, he has hardly put any weight on since he was a teenager. He seems to burn it all off with his active lifestyle. 'Even when I've been rehearsing with Scarlet Division, I still manage to get up at seven in the morning and go on a three- or four-mile jog. I don't belong to a gym because I don't think I would be able to fit it around my work.'

Jamie starts the day with a breakfast of his favourite natural muesli but he confesses, 'I also have a passion for bacon sandwiches.' He hardly ever just sits down and unwinds. 'It's difficult, because I am a naturally hyperactive person,' he says. 'But I do like to watch some telly and listen to music with Jools. And we often go out for a meal. I like to be waited on and enjoy other people's cooking.'

But he is careful about what he eats, 'It's not so much what I don't eat, as how a thing is cooked. I won't eat anything that is deep fried or greasy. That's not healthy at all. And I wouldn't want to serve it up for anyone else either. I am not that careful about what I eat. I believe in everything in moderation and a little bit of what you fancy doing you good. I eat lots of fruit and salads because I like them and I try to avoid the fatty stuff wherever possible.

'I never take any vitamin or mineral pills,

because I think they are a load of old rubbish. If you eat a balanced diet you will be fine. I am lucky, I never go to the doctor, I don't catch colds in winter and I don't think I suffer from stress.

'I don't really do anything to look after my skin. I don't use creams or anything, just my hands. I don't even use soap half the time. I can manage fairly happily on four or five hours' sleep a night which is helpful when calls start coming in from America and Australia in the middle of the night. But I find it hard to get up in the morning and I always struggle to stay in as long as possible. When I lived at home, my dad used to get me up with a squirt from the hosepipe when he was watering the garden.'

Jamie does have one favourite alternative therapy that never fails to make him feel better – lying flat out like a cat and having his back gently scratched by Jools. 'It always works,' says Jamie. When he looks in the mirror, Jamie says he thinks, What an ugly bastard. 'People say I am a pin-up but I don't believe a word of it.'

Ever approachable Jamie has good advice when the questions are serious. How can I get protein-rich dishes without meat?

'To be honest, when you have got specific dietary problems it is such a bore as it affects your life. So the best thing I suggest is to spend £50 on a dietician who can write down everything you can and cannot eat. It will really transform the way you eat as they give you all sorts of help and advice on where to buy stuff. The biggest fact about cooking is that you do not have to be rich to eat well. All the best cooking in the world is from peasant culture and all those really cheap bits of meat like chicken drumsticks are so fantastic to cook with and they don't break the bank. I will have a kids section in my next book. A lot of people have written about kids from a parent's perspective but I have written it for the parents from the eyes of a seven-year-old and what they want to do and there are a lot of things that kids can do in cookery.

'To make up recipes all the time you have to be a bit mad. Chatting to people tends to inspire me to go off and pull something together. It is important to use a good knife to cut with. Globals are pretty good, but then Gustaff, Henkles, Victorian Ox and Sabatier are all very good. You get what you pay for at the end of the day.'

Jamie regards students with particular affection. After all, it is not so long ago that he was one of them. He advises, 'If you are a student, anything you cook for your girlfriend will impress her. Normally in student towns there are good markets.

If you go to the markets on a Friday you can get some really good prices on meat so it becomes affordable. Try something a little bit different, something Italian or Thai so you don't have to fill yourself up too much. A good Thai green curry or a really nice roast with anything seasonal such as asparagus or broad beans in spring. Because they are seasonal, they will be reasonably priced.

'I cook offal all the time. There are some amazing Italian pastas made from all those offal cuts. If we knew what was in it we wouldn't eat it, but if it is chopped up enough we don't notice! I have got a friend who owns a restaurant and he does some amazing things like steamed and fried pig's ear with pesto and some really mad stuff that you have to be a foodie to like. Offal is completely under-rated.

'The most unusual place I have ever cooked was either Number 10 Downing Street or on the end of Southend Pier with a gas burner. It was a very nice kitchen at Number 10 and it was very clean.

'I think there is a very bright future for British meat and English produce on the whole, actually. We have had so many knocks over the years but we have come back from it. Sometimes you need a knock to sort you back out again. The fact that people take notice of where things come from now is very good. It is hard when I travel; I get fed up with foreigners making fun of British cooking.'

Jamie is determined to stay true to his roots and is fiercely unpretentious. He insists, 'I have not got a "signature dish". I am too young and too curious.'

But there are things he really will not eat. 'I really hate eating bulls' testicles. I don't want to eat them, even though they are on a couple of top menus at the moment.' And if he could choose a star couple to grace his table, 'I would like to cook for Jay Kay and Kate Winslet. I think they would make a very good dinner party couple.

'There is no one sort of food I enjoy. I enjoy everything. The world is your oyster.'

Jamie is not upset if people burp after eating one of his meals. So long are they are friends. 'If I know them, I think it is hilarious. If I don't know them, I think it is rude. But if the burp has real depth, I do appreciate it.'

The worst person Jamie has ever had to cook for is Harvey Keitel, because he wanted to write his own menu. 'When we gave him a perfect spaghetti arrabiate he kept sending it back saying it wasn't cooked properly. We should have sent him out some Tabasco or a Pot Noodle!'

Asked to name three famous people he would like to cook for, Jamie said, 'No one excites me that much. I like cooking for real people, not buffed-up famous Hollywood stars. I would be just as happy cooking for Andy my gas man and Sheila Alum our local gypsy. She is a beautiful woman and she likes potato picking. She is a spud basher.'

'The three herbs I couldn't live without are thyme because it is sexy, basil because it is sexy, and rosemary because it is sexy. My favourite condiment is balsamic vinegar. You can use it in loads of things. You can get expensive stuff that is a real luxury or cheap stuff that just tastes nicer than normal vinegar. You can use it in salads and you can use it in stews and even in desserts.

'Gennaro could replace me for one episode of my programme because he is a great cook and a great laugh but I think he would have to be about 25 years younger.

'It is absolutely fantastic knowing that lots of people use my recipes. Especially when it is little kids doing the cooking, which I think is the best thing in the world.

'Cooking is not rocket science, it is just common sense. I can't touch Delia. She is the boss. Everyone wants me to slag off Gordon Ramsay and Delia to get headlines but I really think they are incredibly talented.'

But eating out brings out the oddest quirks in

people. Jamie says, 'The strangest complaint I have ever had in any restaurant I was working in was that our portions were too generous!'

Chapter Ten

Local Hero to Global Star

Jamie is fortunate to enjoy very good health. He is proud of not having taken a day off ill in over six years of working. He used to work hard to keep in shape by taking regular cross-country runs but nowadays his most energetic exercise is his drumming. His favourite drummer is Steve Gadd. And his hobbies are drumming and coarse fishing.

Jamie regrets not paying more attention at school in his English lessons and happily admits that he would find it an awful lot easier to write if he had tried harder. He reckons one of his great strengths is getting things done and not waiting for events to happen.

As for ambitions, Jamie is aiming high. 'I would like to win a Michelin star, but it is unlikely. My cooking just isn't fiddly enough and that is fine by me. Half of these £100-a-head places aren't half as good as the stuff my old dad serves up by the fire with a pint of Guinness for £8.

'I want to live in a little village on the outskirts of Cambridge and have my own restaurant, with Jools doing the front of house. I can't wait, I want to be like Rick Stein. He has been in the business for ever and is still fanatical about food. The main thing is to keep cooking well and explain it clearly.

'Cambridge is quaint and quiet with a really good market but a shortage of good restaurants. I want to open a restaurant with a deli, even with a fishmonger's and a butcher's.'

But Cambridge is an expensive place to set up a restaurant, particularly with some of the rents being set by the universities, in some cases becoming extremely prohibitive. 'As a result,' says Jamie warming to his theme, 'Cambridge is in danger of becoming bland like every other boring, overspill city, full of high street chains and unexciting restaurants. I want to get a vibe happening and create something fresh, some-thing new and trendy, but they are just selling out to the big boys who can afford the rents. We are now looking at a few villages outside Cambridge and I have also decided to look in Brighton. I would like to live near the sea. Whatever happens, I want to get out of London. I'm a country boy really.'

On the financial side, Jamie and Jools paid £500,000 for their latest love-nest. Jamie turned down an offer from the government to be the new hospital food tsar. Loyd Grossman got the job.

Jamie did not make an instant fortune from his sudden burst of fame. He received £2,000 an episode and reckoned in the six months of filming that he could have made far more money from working his shifts in The River Café kitchens.

And he felt he did not get a good deal from the first book contracts signed for *The Naked Chef* cookbook. 'It costs £18.99 and I get something like 70p per book.'

At that early stage, he simply thought the fame would pass quickly through his life and provide some welcome publicity for the restaurant he planned to open within the next 18 months.

Jamie said before fame arrived, 'It is just a question of finding the right premises. I have already got the financial backing and lots of ideas. I also want to have my own butcher's and delicatessen eventually, making sure that I can get a really good supply of the kind of fresh organic, free-range ingredients that I need. That is what real cooking should be about, getting the right food and cooking it as little as possible. I can't bear all this fiddling around with tiny bits of leaves on plates and people holding them up and breathing over them until they look right. I hate that style of regimented cooking. I could never have worked in a kitchen where I was screamed at all the time and made to do things all one way. That is why I loved it at The River Café. There, we used ingredients in season, at their freshest, and changed the menu twice a day. I hate the idea of serving something like asparagus in January and then having to fly it in from Morocco.'

Jamie Oliver soon proved that his popularity was international. The originality and freshness of *The Naked Chef* has made it one of the BBC's most successful television exports. It is now screened in more than 50 countries worldwide and the list is growing all the time. The BBC report that the series is popular from New York to New Zealand and countless outposts in between. Israeli television audiences are particularly turned on to the show and have pushed it to the top of the ratings, and even

Finding time to fundraise.

Left: Having fun with Chef Delia Smith at the annual Jamie Oliver Foundation fundraiser in 2010.

© *Rex Features*

Below: Supporting Red Nose Day in 2001.

© *Rex Features*

SAY PANTS TO PO

Extending his brand name by promoting his monthly food magazine, *Jamie*, in 2008.

© Rex Feat

mie's not afraid to poke fun while raising awareness. A 'fat' Jamie promoting his *Back School Dinners* television programme in 2006.

© *Rex Features*

Right: The 2005 National TV Awards was a cause of celebration for Jamie after winning the Special Recognition Award and Best Factual Programme for *Jamie's School Dinners*.   © *Rex Features*

Below: Getting further recognition for *Jamie's School Dinners* in 2006. Jamie posing with his BAFTA for Best Factual Series.   © *Rex Features*

haps the best accolade of them all. Jamie collecting his MBE medal at Buckingham
lace in 2003. Controversially, Jamie didn't wear a tie!

© Rex Features

Above: Jamie takes the time to relax at his flagship Fifteen restaurant in London.

© Rex Featu

Below: Jamie on the beach with his trainee chefs at the third Fifteen restaurant in Cornwa

© Rex Featu

ove: Jamie giving his verdict on school dinners in his battle to change kids' diets for
: better in *Jamie's School Dinners*.

© *Rex Features*

low: Spreading the word and the food: dishing out healthy school dinners in Leicester
uare, London.

© *Rex Features*

Above: Rubbing shoulders with royalty – and not for the first or last time! The Prince of Wales and Duchess of Cornwall listen to Jamie, accompanied by his favourite dinner lady, Norah Sands.

© PA Pho

Below: Jamie's role as guardian angel of our children's health is complete, as he meets with Tony Blair, then Prime Minister, to secure a new funding package for school dinners.

© PA Pho

countries famed for their culinary excellence like France and Italy are switching on.

Naturellement, in France the colourful Jamie Oliver commentary was dubbed into the local language and voiced over by a French actor. But the country that frequently seems to believe that it invented food still struggled with Jamie's down-to-earth slang. Evidently, there were no words quite to convey the meaning of 'wicked' and 'pukka' as Jamie delivers them in Britain. But *The Naked Chef* series spearheaded a package of BBC cookery programmes which were sold across the Channel for £5 million.

It was a deal which stunned many French food experts who felt the home of fine cooking hardly needed help from the British. But an expansive BBC spokesman insisted, 'The truth is that things have become stale in the French larder. They are now looking for brighter, bolder talents to revitalise their cooking. They adore Jamie, not just because he is young and good-looking but because he is a fine chef. The French have finally worked out that the British are very good cooks. Perhaps even better than they are. We certainly know more than they do about making cookery fun.'

The BBC shows were bought by the fast-rising new French cookery channel TV Gourmand and the station's managing director, Miriam Duteil, enthused, 'These programmes will be a refreshing change for the French viewer.'

Top Australian journalist Phil Hammond noted the Jamie Oliver impact down under. 'He's suddenly come from nowhere to be just about the most popular chef in Australia,' said Phil. *The Naked Chef* brought record ratings to Channel Two as Jamie's refreshingly enthusiastic approach went down well with Aussie viewers. 'He seems to love what he is doing in the kitchen and the food looks great,' said Phil. 'In spite of what some people might think, there is a lot more to Australian cuisine than throwing another prawn on the barbie, but we can still learn from Jamie. I tried one of his roast lamb recipes when we had some friends round and it went down really well. I even tried to cook naked once but my wife told me to put my clothes right back on again and our dog Chad just about howled the place down.'

The Naked Chef is a smash hit in the United States on the Food Network as Jamie Oliver has succeeded where an earlier export, Ainsley Harriott, failed dismally.

'Ainsley swept off to a good start,' said a Los Angeles television producer. 'And he had very good figures for a while. But gradually viewers seemed to find his eccentricity was phoney and as soon as the audience starts to believe you're not genuine, you're sunk. With Jamie, even when they couldn't understand what he was saying, they loved him. That little-boy-lost look went down a storm and, boy, that guy knows his onions and all the rest of the vegetables.'

Jamie's Los Angeles-based producer Lance Reynolds said that Jamie was being treated like a rock star but the adulation was having little effect. 'It may be exhausting, but it is not changing him. He is still just a bloke.' Reynolds noted that 'Oliver fever' had started to build even before Jamie arrived, after the influential *Rolling Stone* magazine named the British chef as its 'millennial man to watch', and *People* magazine named him just behind Brad Pitt in its poll of sexy men.

It seemed that Jamie revived almost single-handedly the British cookery invasion that had been floundering in the doldrums for so long.

The programme director of the Food Network, Bruce Seidel, was certain Jamie was going to become a major star. 'He is youthful,' said Seidel. 'He appeals to young and old, and to men and women, and he is very rock 'n' roll. He works well on our television and seems to charm everyone who sees him, unlike Delia Smith who is perhaps a bit too old school for Americans.'

Five years earlier, British cuisine was regarded as a joke by most Americans, but now cooking from Britain has become fashionable. 'We want as much British culinary talent as we can get over here.'

The Food Network recruited Ross Burden from *Ready Steady Cook!* to film an introduction to British cuisine called *Tasting England* and has revived programmes made by the two Fat Ladies and even rerun the '70s favourite Graham Kerr, the Galloping Gourmet. Ainsley's show was cut short in September 2000 when NBC cancelled his highly-promoted cookery-cum-talk show, but following the impact of Jamie, the Harriott US television profile was revamped rather than quietly terminated.

The new British invasion was inspired and greatly helped by an enormous growth of interest in good food among American people, which was sparked by greater affluence, an increase in foreign travel and the spread of cheap but high-quality restaurants which have brought more adventurous food to a wider number of people.

'It owes more to Sir Terence Conran and the Gap than to French *haute cuisine*,' said Los Angeles-based food industry analyst Rob Glassier. 'People want something between burgers and something scary in a fruit sauce. The new chefs, including Jamie Oliver, are pathfinding that.'

American writers could not praise Jamie too highly. 'This boy-man is to the food industry what Robbie Williams is to Brit-rock,' said one syndicated columnist. 'He's taken the restaurant scene by storm with his major cooking series on TV.'

Jamie was crowned the sexiest chef by influential *People* magazine. But he tried to impress upon the American public that he and Jools were not the wild socialites some viewers might have imagined. 'We are just a couple of very boring people. We are like homebodies.'

Even the toughest interviewers seemed to melt before Jamie's natural charm. The Americans even quizzed him on mad cow disease and he responded, 'I can honestly say that as a chef, mad cow disease has been the best thing to happen in my career. It has forced farmers to answer tough questions and offer even tougher regulations to this industry. But then any ingredient I use in my cooking, from herbs to meats and in between, is organic and that includes my beef.'

Jamie was so busy he had two personal assistants to juggle the endless demands on his time. 'I had to get help. We were working 16- and 17-hour days and I was just beat.'

The pressure grew and grew and, in an unguarded moment, Jamie bleated, 'Everyone wants a part of me. I really feel like a piece of meat.' It was a quote that was to come back and haunt him but, in fact, he soon recovered his lack of sleep and relaunched himself into the fray. But he was right – a lot of the female half of America did appear to be lusting after Jamie Oliver as if he were just a piece of meat. The Food Network realised even before transmission had started that they had something special in *The Naked Chef*, and to ensure their viewers understood some of the more uniquely Essex words that Jamie uses they provided a special translation guide. According to the Food Network, 'lovely jubbly' meant 'really nice', 'pukka' meant 'excellent', 'whizz it' meant 'mix together', 'wicked' meant 'cool' and 'malarkey' translated as 'blah, blah, blah'. Never were two countries more comprehensively divided by a common language you might think.

A Food Network insider revealed that the women in the organisation were already highly taken with the newcomer. 'I don't know what it is about Jamie, but they have really taken to him, even before his show starts. We saw his show when we were in Britain and loved it. The guy is a complete natural. He is like one of your cute young Brit pop stars. We couldn't understand what he was saying but I don't think the girls will be complaining too much. Girls think he is sexy and their moms want to mother him.'

Jamie went down a storm when he followed up the Regis Philbin appearance by going on the hugely popular *Today* show. The majority of the studio audience of the NBC show were young women and they watched enthralled as the cheeky chappie dressed in the scruffy Space Invader T-shirt and jeans chatted about himself and his food as if he did not have a care in the world.

New York Times fashion editor Libby Callaway was among them and she instantly became one of the newest members of Jamie's fan club. Libby could scarcely believe her eyes. She said, 'He is lovely. He is going to be a huge hit with all the women in New York. We love that accent and the fact that he is so young. He seems like a bit of a naughty boy and he charms the camera so brilliantly, I think he is just what we want to brighten up the American food scene.'

British fashion writer Anna Gizowska had just moved to work in New York and she said, 'I have only been in the States for two weeks and the only guy people are talking about at parties is Jamie Oliver. As soon as I got here, sophisticated women in fancy cocktail dresses were sidling up to me and saying, "Do you know Jamie Oliver? Have you interviewed him before?" I was thinking, Get real, he's just a scruffy British chef.'

Jamie was contrasted with Ainsley Harriott whose show preceded *The Naked Chef* to America. Harriott had gone down well at first, but the market research came in to reveal that a lot of women found his camp style slightly confusing and Jamie was not remotely camp. An observer said, 'Ainsley is kinda weird but Jamie is so cute. He is the guy all my friends want to get in a corner at a bar or a nightclub. Most Americans have the view that British food is bland and unappealing. But if this chef is as good as he looks, I think we will change our view a little.'

And it was not just the women who took notice. Influential *New York Post* columnist Neil Travis revealed that food watchers had been buzzing about Jamie Oliver's arrival in the United States for months. He reckoned that hip, handsome and happening Jamie was being called the Guy Ritchie of the kitchen – lock, stock and two simmering saucepans. The word was that Madonna is a big fan of the young chef's natural charm.

American journalists probed hard to see if that easy-going attitude was more than skin deep. But Jamie did not join the usual moans about the price of fame and shrugged off the problems of living with celebrity status. When the *Los Angeles Times* pushed him on the subject, he said fame was experiencing a guy jumping out of a Jeep with a camera with a big lens and snapping a picture. 'He looked like a guy with a problem, then you find yourself in the papers. It's not a big deal,' said Jamie.

Jamie told the Americans how a mention of vanilla pods in an early programme caused a run on them in Britain and he enthused about teaching people to be more discerning in their shopping. 'No one should accept bad spinach from their grocery store,' he insisted.

The Food Network knew they had something special when they launched Jamie Oliver as The Naked Chef. Cleverly, they teased the public into taking a look to see if he really was naked on screen and took huge billboards and bus shelter ads across America to announce their new star. Jools enthused, 'In Times Square in New York they have erected a huge poster of *The Naked Chef* and it depicts nothing more than a suggestively peeled banana. So, obviously, the Americans have got a sense of humour.' The radio campaign was particularly provocative as a sexy woman's voice purred tantalisingly about 'a red juicy strawberry pressed against longing lips'.

But it turned out that the hype was hardly needed. The show was so good that the word of mouth was sensational. He was instantly invited back on *Today* after his flirting with Katie. CBS called him to explore ideas for a sitcom. ABC wanted a meeting and there's a fortune to be made from syndication. The Food Network insists it is in discussions with him about other projects. And, ingenuously, Jamie said he was happy to consider all offers and proposals but he did have his own agenda which is a future with Jools and their children, and running a single 'genius' restaurant outside London. He made jaws drop in the studios when he said, 'I'm really not here to break America like a lot of pop stars. It's just cooking.'

Jamie toured the country signing books, appearing on endless radio and TV talk shows and explaining a million times that he would not actually be appearing naked himself. *USA Today*'s Ellen Hale reported that Jamie's gusto and genuine enthusiasm for food was what produced the 'nearly overnight success which has turned him into a global television personality and bestselling cookbook author, and an immediate smash in the USA where he hit the ground running and hasn't stopped'.

Jamie's books, *The Naked Chef* and *The Return of the Naked Chef*, have sold three million copies around the world. The first one swept to number one on the San Francisco bestseller list much to Jamie's astonishment. 'I had never even been there,' he said. 'It ridiculous, just ridiculous.'

Americans loved Jamie's unstuffy, no-nonsense style of cooking and he was quickly nominated for a top television cooking award. He sparkled away happily on chat shows hosted by Regis Philbin, Jay Leno, David Letterman, Rosie O'Donnell and Katie Couric just for starters and he had to explain to every one of them that it was the food that was stripped down and not the presenter.

The advertisers were especially delighted because Jamie drew in audiences right across the demographic range, young and old, rich and poor, even male and female were all very well represented. Jamie kept laughing off the old gay icon line and was genuinely pleased that men were switching on with their womenfolk. He said, 'A successful cookbook must involve a lot of men getting in touch with their feminine side.'

'His passion for food is so infectious,' says Eileen Opatur, the chief programmer at the Food Network, trying to explain Jamie Oliver's popularity. 'He has no inhibitions when it comes to making it, talking about it and eating it.'

And Bobby Ray, who was once a young TV star chef himself and is now executive chef of the New York restaurants Mesa Grill and Bolo, said, 'Jamie seems to be the perfect answer for Generation X cooking enthusiasts. He is a rock star who cooks. That is what it comes down to.'

Canada was just as quick as the United States to switch on to *The Naked Chef*. Jody Read, acquisitions programmer for TV Ontario, first saw Jamie Oliver on screen at the Cannes television convention in 1999. She said, 'I had gone to see Optomen, producers of the *Two Fat Ladies*, about following up on their next series. And they were also in the process of producing six episodes of a new show called *The Naked Chef* and they showed me a clip.' One sight of that lithe young body sliding down his spiral staircase and enthusing over the leg of lamb in the first programme was enough for Jody. 'I thought Jamie was wonderful. I found him extremely engaging. His love of cooking is very contagious. I ran out and bought a leg of lamb and cooked it for my family.'

New Zealand produced the same ecstatic reaction to *The Naked Chef*. One minute he was totally unknown, and the next he was on everyone's lips. All critics loved his show and the ratings built rapidly. One quoted an early British review, 'Jamie Oliver looks like a rock star, sounds like a yob and cooks like an angel.' And how true it was.

But Jamie pointed out that there were penalties to being a successful television chef. 'If I go round to somebody's house for a posh dinner, say, and they just give me a bacon sandwich, well, I'd love it if it was good. But if they just give me any old thing then we will all have a laugh about it. But the thing is, when you are a chef on telly and your book is at number one then you do find that the offers dwindle slightly. People are scared to cook for you.' But if Jools knocks out some fish fingers, potatoes and peas late at night, then I'm a happy boy, aren't I?'

New Zealand really liked Jamie and his uncompromisingly fresh approach. Writer Christopher Moore raved, 'Jamie Oliver demystifies and demythologises decades of pretentious culinary preciousness.'

Jamie really liked New Zealand as well, and while out there promoting his book he spent some time with some very hospitable Maori folk who were keen to show him some of their traditional cooking methods. They were particularly proud of their ancient method of cooking underground. Jamie was fascinated.

'They dig a pit, light a fire in it and chuck in a load of big fat rocks. They let them get really hot, then they take half the rocks out, put a whole goat or a wild boar on top of the rest, put the hot rocks back over the top and cover the whole lot with earth. Half a day later, they come back and dinner is ready. That is, if they can remember where they buried it.'

Jamie decided that some primitive Maori cooking was just the way to celebrate the birthday of his old friend Jimmy. Jamie draped the Maori greenstone he had been given in New Zealand round his neck to get himself in the mood and, with another friend called Andy, they began digging a hole in Jimmy's garden.

Considering that the last time they had lit a fire near Jimmy's had been when the trio were at junior school – and that time they managed to set fire to a strip of dried-out grass half the size of a football pitch – this was an enterprising culinary adventure to say the least. The three old friends found it much harder than the Maoris seemed to and even tried using an old parrot cage inside the pit. Eventually, they somehow managed to cook salmon, pheasants, chicken drumsticks and suckling pig and it turned into a luscious feast. Remarkably, they managed without setting fire to any of the countryside and with the aid of a liberal seasoning of lager and beer. The end result was brilliant, insisted Jamie, though the exact procedure is unlikely to feature in any future *Naked Chef* books!

Jamie found himself in some strange situations as he flew round the globe turning *The Naked Chef* into an international hero. His enthusiasm for food always leads him to be happy to try the most outlandish dishes, but he almost drew the line in Japan where he arrived to promote the TV show. His hosts wanted to show him how honoured they were to receive such an esteemed guest and pushed the boat out by serving up cod semen. 'And, of course, because I was the guest, I got the biggest bit,' he gulped.

Jamie's success in America turned him into a phenomenon almost overnight. But not without upsetting some of the United States' more traditional cooks. They carped at his populist recipes and sneered at the Oliver-style of cookery as over-hyped and under-nourished. They accused him of pandering to those who wanted to dumb down American cuisine. Judith Graham, the owner of Bistro 2000 in the centre of Chicago, could understand the appeal of Jamie and admitted, 'He is cute, which is why the networks will gobble him up, like they did the Beatles or Oasis,' she said. 'But some of his stripped-down recipes reduce good food to banal mash. Too many of his creations are overheated, under-nourished rubbish.'

And the eminent Claude Segal, who earned two Michelin stars in Paris before taking over the Sunset Room in Los Angeles, was even less impressed. He said, 'It is very fashionable, but in inexperienced hands it can ruin more dishes than it improves, making food far too sweet. I shall not be watching this *Naked Chef*. It is entertainment, not cooking.'

But the viewers thought very differently. When the first 'Americanised' edition of *The Naked Chef* was broadcast on the New York-based Food Network, the producers took the precaution of editing out some of Jamie's more impenetrable expressions. It was considered that American viewers would have difficulty in understanding the meaning of 'lovely jubbly' in spite of the qualified success on the other side of the Atlantic of John Sullivan's wonderful comedy *Only Fools and Horses*. And the excitingly expressive 'whizz it' was another phrase that was drastically reduced in number. Not only that, but the cable network also took the unusual step of including a Cockney dictionary on its promotional website.

Jamie wanted the American launch to be taken seriously and he put in several weeks of promotional effort which was greeted with a terrific reaction from American viewers. He made a string of exhausting appearances on daytime chat shows in both New York and Los Angeles, which clearly paid off as his début was watched by around 11 million people, a new record for a food programme shown on American television.

The Americans were not slow to appreciate Jamie's sex appeal. And many of the female television critics were openly disappointed that he did not quite live up to the programme's title. 'Jamie Oliver brings out what I shall delicately describe as my maternal instinct,' said one correspondent from Ohio wistfully.

Jamie's book started to comfortably outsell more politically-correct cookbooks like *The Soul of a Chef*, *The Low Carb Cookbook* and Deborah

Madison's California hit of the year *This Can't Be Tofu*.

Typically, Jamie said he was simply 'gobsmacked' by the attention he received in America. He was openly followed down the streets by teenage girls, who made it clear that it was his body rather than his cooking skills that they were interested in testing. Three older fans had to be ejected by security men from the ABC television studios when he was being interviewed by quiz show host Regis Philbin.

Two up-market New York hookers strolled up to the reception desk at Jamie's hotel anxious to gain access to his room. A startled night manager could not believe the women's unashamed determination to see Jamie. 'They were tall and elegant and beautiful-looking girls and they just smiled and said that they wanted to give Jamie their own special version of a welcome to America,' said the hotel worker. 'I must have looked a bit surprised and they spelled it out for me. "We want to ball his brains out, baby. That guy is so cute we want to give him the best freebie he's ever had."

'I spluttered that this offer was quite out of the question, and they said if I could fix it to get inside his suite, they would fix me up first. The two girls on reception thought it was hilarious when I went bright red with embarrassment but I called security and had them ejected. I've never seen anything like it in ten years in the business.'

Chapter Eleven

Boiling Point

By early 2001, the relentless rise and rise of Jamie Oliver the television sensation was beginning to take its toll on our hero. The very thought of getting stale and repetitive horrified the energetic chef. He and Jools talked long into the night about the pressure on their lives and their lack of time alone and they decided together that Jamie needed to move on and develop his talents more widely. There would be just one more series of *The Naked Chef* for the BBC they decided, and then they would take much more control of their lives.

With characteristic openness, Jamie revealed he would complete the third series and no more. He said frankly, 'I have had an amazing two-and-a-half years, but I need to take some time off and step back from the spotlight for a bit. I think I am in danger of people getting sick of me.'

Jamie was not surprised that his distinctive style of show was being copied by many other people and was honest enough to admit that his programmes were no longer quite so special.

The vast commercial potential of Jamie Oliver was thrown into the sharpest focus when the charismatic chef decided it was time he took more control of his own future. After a huge bidding war, Jamie announced in April 2001 that he would be leaving the BBC to set up his own production company, Fresh Productions. He struck a multi-million-pound deal with Pearson TV, the television giant behind screen favourites like *The Bill* and *Neighbours*. Jamie owned 75 per cent of the new company with Pearson holding the rest.

Jamie was keen to take care of his long-term financial future and also to develop his own talents behind as well as in front of the cameras. The tabloids announced that Jamie would be 'the new Chris Evans', which had the chef remarking that he hoped they were referring to the Evans business success rather than his colourfully unconventional private life. Jamie said he was over the moon and could not wait to get started on the new phase of his life. 'This is a great opportunity for me to be really creative and explore television cookery. I can't wait to get started.'

Jamie was buzzing with ideas for new cutting-edge and original shows and Jools was closely involved with the plan. 'The more it enables us to work together, the better,' said Jamie. 'We want to get involved with new areas of television like music, nature and fashion, not just cookery.'

In February 2001, the papers reported that Jamie and Jools were to move to the United States for at least six months. He was grabbed at the British Book Awards in London and advised reporters that he was keen to satisfy the American hunger for a taste of the Naked Chef. He was quoted as saying, 'There are not enough hours in the day to satisfy the Americans, so I have got to go there for half a year.'

Reports that Jamie was going to live in the United States for six months were wrong. 'No, it was just that journalists kept asking me what I was doing in America and I said everything was going very well,' said Jamie. 'I am out there once a month as I have got a show out there. I said that if I wanted it to work really well out there, I would have to move out there for six months, but I didn't exactly say I was going to move there.'

Whichever way it goes, it is unlikely that Jamie will ever start taking himself too seriously with his campaign of global domination. The American series has an audience of 11 million and is growing all the time. Jamie laughed, 'They are mad for the show. The only trouble is that they don't understand a word that I say.'

Fame does tend to breed jealousy and Jamie has been the subject of some unkind rumours. A suspicion began to emerge that his accent might not be entirely his own, that he might be a public school boy slumming it. That's rubbish. For most of Jamie's childhood, he lived above a pub, The Cricketers, and he went to the local state school.

Round his neck Jamie wears a silver chain inscribed with the words 'Jamie – Love You Always', a gift from his Jools that he treasures. Jamie Oliver is not a secret toff. What you see is what you get.

'I think I'm pretty much the same geezer as I am on telly,' he insists. 'My parents come from Southend. They speak quite well, but they are nowhere near posh. My mates came from West Ham, Chingford, and two of them were gyppos from the village.'

And now he really seems to have become the new Delia Smith. Is he still a fan? Although her food might not be Jamie's sort of thing, he still has a mighty high regard for her work. 'Any woman who can sustain her career for 25 years has got to be a genius,' he says. 'Her food is the kind of food my mum cooks and, most importantly, she writes recipes that are accessible at the supermarket.'

Jamie is modest about his own achievements. Of his television work, he says, 'I just open my mouth and out it comes. Y'know,' he adds, 'I was walking along Hatton Garden when this dirty-looking builder yelled out to me, "Oi, Jamie, I made that risotto and it was brilliant." That sort of thing's amazing. I'm chuffed. Over the moon.'

As far as relaxing at home goes, Jamie and Jools seem to have found the perfect blend for a happy marriage – compromise. 'My wife Jools and I have very different tastes in movies, so we tend to squabble over the video. She likes chick flicks and tacky '80s romances, while I prefer sci-fi and gangster films. My favourites are definitely the *Star Wars* and *Alien* films. We did both enjoy Woody Allen's *Small-time Crooks* and Guy Ritchie's *Snatch*. Brad Pitt is such a professional. He had his Irish accent down pat and some of the people who worked with him told me that he didn't expect any special Hollywood treatment.'

Jamie keeps pretty unsocial hours so he watches a lot of TV on video. 'On a night off, it is bliss to veg out on the sofa in front of Alan Partridge or Ali G. I have a penchant for Open University programmes as well, and Jools often catches me on the sofa at two in the morning glued to a programme about internal combustion engines.'

It is not easy to balance family life with the pressures of such a busy working schedule. 'I don't know how I work it out really,' says Jamie. 'I just get on with it. I think everyone thinks I am on television quite a lot but really apart from the adverts it is only about four hours a year. Because the books are so popular and I get asked to do things like The Brits, it seems like I do more than I do. I get on with a normal life really and the nice thing is that I am known for being myself so people are quite nice when I meet them.'

Jamie has met lots of interesting people but he takes people at face value and is never impressed simply by fame and reputation. He says, 'The writer Richard Curtis is probably the most interesting person I have met so far. I am not sure why, he is just an interesting bloke. He is the guy who wrote *Blackadder* and *Notting Hill* among other things. You can't help but respect him, especially for his involvement in Comic Relief which is so important to him he puts it before offers from Hollywood sometimes.'

And Jamie's not averse to building a reputation as a culinary agony-uncle to the rich and famous. He got a real kick when Fatboy Slim phoned to ask if it was all right to use shark instead of tuna in one of his recipes. 'And it is – it sounded like he was doing a good job,' said Jamie.

But as for his own Hollywood aspirations, Jamie is philosophical – and dismissive of 'hype' generally. 'People tend not to recognise me in the street that much because, basically, I am just a scruffy git,' says Jamie.

But some strange incidents have marked his short but heady spell of fame. 'One of the weirdest was getting knickers sent through the post,' says Jamie. He's also had to adjust to such eventualities as 'going to the supermarket and finding every other person looking round the corner and through gaps in the shelves to see what I have got in my trolley. And trying not to be shocked when hairy middle-aged women think it is all right to give you a kiss!'

Jamie was delighted to be asked with Jools to present an award at The Brits. 'Jools was excited and I thought it was pretty cool. I am in a band and have been since I was 13 so it was nice to be at the big awards. I presented one of the first awards and by the time I got out, the event was nearly over so viewers probably had a better view at home.

'Personality-wise, I don't think fame has affected me but I do think that as soon as you realise you are bit of a commodity, you have to become a bit of a businessman quite quickly.'

But the pressure on Jamie to do more and more things is relentless. On Christmas Day 2000, Jamie and Jools split themselves in two. Jools said that they both had new nephews and they wanted to see them open their presents but they all got together later. She did say that Jamie was so busy working that she had to book a table at the restaurant to get to see him. 'Jamie is working harder than ever,' she said. 'I am so proud of him but I do miss him.'

Jools tries hard to keep her husband sane and to protect him from the endless demands on his time. It is a constant battle and occasionally she puts her pretty foot down. Jamie tried to explain, 'Look, darling, it's for our future,' but she said she had had enough. 'So now I do everything I can to make sure we have at least every Sunday together. We just chill out and that day is like an oasis of peace in my crazy life.'

Jamie knows the fame is not going to last for ever at this level and he is delighted about that. The spotlight can become permanently dazzling if you stay in it for too long. In six years, he plans to be off to the country where he will 'open a pub, grow my own food, have a donkey and some chickens and close at the weekends'.

Jamie Oliver did not set out to be a star. Growing up, he and his friends were all the 'thick bastards' at school. After he became a success, he felt like writing his English teacher a letter and getting all the spelling wrong. 'When I am an old geezer, I might consider opening up a cookery school. I am too busy at the moment,' says the international TV star, bestselling author – and pukka cook.

Chapter Twelve

Hoisting the Sales

Jamie Oliver does not allow his name to be used by a company lightly or without getting fully involved in the project. Jamie had turned down out of hand an approach to pose naked with a can of Coca-Cola and to promote Nescafé. But when he agreed to become the new 'face' of Sainsbury's, he made sure there was a full and frank exchange of views in June 2000 with the supermarket chain's distinguished chief executive Sir Peter Davies.

Jamie said afterwards, 'Sir Peter spent five minutes telling me about his vision for the future, then I said to him, "This is my baby, too, you know. Your hassle is my hassle." '

The businessman smiled genially and realised that there was more to the young chef than his high-spirited television image.

The cynics were swift to scoff, but Jamie was being honest when he insisted that he agreed to get involved with Sainsbury's so he could influence the giant grocer for the good, to improve the quality of its food. 'I didn't do it for the money,' said Jamie. 'I did because it gave me a chance to be creative and proactive.'

The opportunity to encourage a supermarket to offer better food – not to mention the lure of around £1 million – seemed too good a chance to miss. 'We're together for the next two years on this one – unless I get on his nerves or he gets on mine,' he says of Sir Peter. 'And I don't think that's going to happen.'

Jamie was frustrated that his local Sainsbury's did not provide all the ingredients for his recipes so he thought by getting directly involved he could improve things. Jamie agreed to front a series of adverts as well as to develop new recipes for the supermarket chain over a two-year deal.

Part of his role – as he sees it – will be to persuade Sainsbury's to sell more organic food. He is very keen on all that organic malarkey. 'As a chef, ingredients are everything,' he says in his high-speed vocal style. 'If you're a car mechanic and you're passionate about it, you go for classic cars, Ferraris; you're not going to be servicing a Skoda. There's no turn-on from that.'

The Sainsbury's adverts put much more work into his busy schedule. The first one was filmed during an all-night session at a London branch just before Jamie got married. How does he manage?

'Chefs have always worked long hours,' he shrugged. He says he is hyperactive, which is just as well. Despite all the temptations of that lovely grub, he is a good 6ft and as lean as he was at 18.

But the high-profile link with Sainsbury's was not without its problems. Jamie was helped into the headlines at a BBC press launch by outspoken Clarissa Dickson-Wright. The surviving half of the Two Fat Ladies attracted press attention when she started spelling out her case against supermarkets and the relationship they have with struggling British agriculture. She said, 'I don't sell out – like certain chefs. I have turned down hundreds of thousands of pounds. My attitude has always been resolutely anti-supermarket.'

Jamie explained that he was also a great supporter of the crucial growers at the sharp end of the industry. Jamie said, 'I do not buy from Sainsbury's for my restaurant. For any chef, supermarkets are like a factory. I buy from specialist growers, organic suppliers and farmers.'

Jamie explained that he advised Sainsbury's on organic suppliers, sourcing chickens and how meat should be hung. But he was not responsible for every nuance of their policy. And Sainsbury's were clearly anxious to calm the situation. A spokesman said, 'We have an excellent relationship with Jamie and supermarkets don't generally supply restaurants, so there is nothing unusual there.'

Jamie's jokey commercials were highly effective, even if they did create the impression that he was hardly off the television. And they were to spark another sharp exchange of views later.

In April 2001, Jamie's highly successful advertising campaign for the supermarket chain upset the BBC when the commercials clashed with his television series. Sainsbury's were forced to re-schedule some of their adverts after it was revealed that a secret agreement had been struck between the company and the BBC to avoid being transmitted on the same evening. The BBC were up in arms when they saw Jamie extolling the virtues of Sainsbury's Blue Parrot Café range of children's meals while the repeats of *The Naked Chef* were running. The BBC seemed to be harking back to the broadcasting attitudes of a bygone age when they said viewers would be 'confused' to see such a popular figure promoting products on one channel while hosting a cookery programme on another.

An unnamed BBC source complained pompously that the clash undermined the integrity of *The Naked Chef* because, to many people, the kitchen in the adverts looks very similar to the one used in the series. The adverts became like an extension to the programme which was the view which did little to endear Jamie to the BBC, especially when the supermarket chain explained that the clash was the fault of the Corporation. Sainsbury's insisted that they had an agreement with the BBC that the adverts would not be transmitted at the same time as the series repeats on the understanding that they received schedules ten weeks in advance of transmission. The BBC failed to provide the necessary notice in time and the company had gone ahead and booked adverts. In the event, Sainsbury's did agree to move some adverts but they were reluctant to lose money over any changes.

Jamie's characteristic honesty got him into the headlines when he cheerfully admitted that he didn't always shop at Sainsbury's himself. Journalists cheerfully swept on to the attack with sneering pieces about Jamie landing 'face-first in the fettuccini'. But Jamie was unruffled. His relationship with Sainsbury's did not mean he had to pledge his life to the supermarket chain. He still had a mind of his own about some of their products. And, unwilling to play the media game, he kept his integrity intact by spelling out his own personal food-buying policy. He said frankly that he was no big fan of the huge 'factory-scale' buying of the larger retailers and that he bought mainly from carefully selected specialist growers, organic suppliers and farmers.

Sainsbury's wisely stepped back from any prospect of a dispute and pointed out that Jamie was speaking about food which he bought for his restaurant. Sainsbury's said they did not normally supply restaurants so there was no problem.

In any case, there are plenty of precedents in which the rich and famous don't always use the products they advertise. A few days earlier, the golf superstar Tiger Woods had confessed that he didn't actually play with the ball he is paid $1 million to endorse. But then the balls he actually uses are so specialised that they are not even available to the general public. Ordinary golfers would, in any case, struggle to control Woods's ball because it requires a special kind of talent. The fans know that they can take or leave the advice they receive from their heroes. The supporters of Manchester United golden boy David Beckham were certainly not disenchanted when, soon after collecting a huge fee from Brylcreem, he treated himself to a skinhead haircut.

Jamie knew that such microscopic scrutiny of his every remark was certain to create headlines but he refused to worry about it. 'I never wanted to be a politician,' he laughed to a friend. 'I say what I honestly feel at the time and if people want to get excited about it then that is up to them. I couldn't give a flying stuff.'

The Sainsbury's ads featuring Jamie, as well as friends and family, have been a huge success and he is in the middle of a two-year contract with them. Sainsbury's are also sponsors of a Happy Days tour which starts in Cambridge at the Corn Exchange and then moves on to the Hammersmith Apollo and then to Australia, New Zealand and South Africa. Jamie plans the ground-breaking events as an action-packed two-hour show which will feature him demonstrating recipes followed by a question-and-answer session with the audience. Jamie says, 'I'll be doing some funky stuff that has never been seen before in a cookery show,' and he promises that there will be thousands of pounds' worth of prizes to be won.

Sainsbury's are delighted with the link with such

a popular personality and they are swamped with requests for Jamie to appear at schools and old people's homes. Especially successful among the ads were Jumbo Fish Fingers from the Blue Parrot Café range, a range of products specifically targeted at children. Thanks to the ad, the fish fingers became a top-selling line.

Jamie took on another lucrative new role when he was appointed consultant chef to Monte's, the uppercrust private members' club in London's Sloane Street which decided to open its door to the public at lunchtime. His former River Café colleague Ben O'Donoghue is head chef and together they have transformed the menus and mood of Monte's restaurant. Jamie has insisted on a typically no-nonsense style of cooking which cleverly combines the best of British with Mediterranean influences.

'I don't actually own the restaurant, but hopefully next year I will open a restaurant, probably with a partner, but we need to find a site first. You can open really small, but if it's really good food you can be really famous and really busy quickly. There are still not that many good people out there. My place won't be mega expensive but not inexpensive, but that is because I want to work with good ingredients.'

Jamie is a great believer in giving value for

money and he gets furious when he finds restaurants or hotels charging a lot for poor service. Jamie and Jools had a night in one of London's swankiest hotels to celebrate his twenty-first birthday. It was a wonderful occasion, right up until the moment they went down to breakfast.

'It was terrible,' remembers Jamie. They were presented with cheap old button mushrooms that had been boiled in a huge pan and came out white with all flavour carefully removed. 'Talk about rubber city,' said Jamie. 'I thought I was chewing a wine gum.'

Jamie loves scrambled eggs and it is such a simple, basic dish he can't understand why so many establishments seem to find it so difficult to prepare. He gets angry when his eggs are so solid they stay in the shape of the serving spoon.

Chapter Thirteen

Success Breeds Success

'I pinch myself every day. I can't believe it is happening,' said Jamie about his sustained success. 'I have had a fantastic response from everyone which is really beautiful but there is a down side. Going to the shops to collect some vegetables used to take me about a quarter-of-an-hour. Now it is an hour or more because loads of people want to speak to me. I don't really mind, but I am really lucky. People seem to be quite positive about me. It would be completely different being a celebrity like Jeremy Beadle who people love to hate.'

Jamie's remarkable popularity seems to go right across the board, to all ages and both sexes. 'People of my own age relate to me and that is good because a lot of younger people are really getting into cooking. It is not just about me, though. I think people in the 35 to 55 age group recognise that my recipes work. If they didn't work, they wouldn't watch the show. The most interesting are people in their seventies and eighties. They love it because they look at me like a grandson. They even tell me I remind them of their own grandsons and sometimes show me pictures. And they usually look nothing like me. What always surprises me is that sometimes the old ladies pinch my bum.'

And the age group Jamie is most interested in appealing to are the children. 'I understand their interest because I was interested when I was a very young child. I am really pleased kids are interested as well. I think that if you can encourage people to cook at an early age, then you set them up with a talent that will be useful all of their life. I like the idea of helping young people. I can imagine them in a few years' time going on to their universities and being able to impress all their mates and do it on a small budget. What could be better than getting a pool of money, buying the ingredients, cooking for 25 people, and then spending the change on beer?'

One of the most endearing aspects of Jamie

Oliver is that fame does not seem to have separated him from his old friends. He refuses to allow his fame and wealth to come between him and childhood chums who are less well known. One of the boys Jamie grew up with in Clavering was Jimmy Doherty who is now a biologist. Jamie says, 'I have known Jimmy since I was two and we have always been close. When we were kids, he was as keen on insects as I was on cooking. The funny thing about Jimmy and me is that we are really alike, but really different. At school we were both pranksters from the word go. The teachers liked us but we never did any decent work. We both had terrible handwriting and could hardly spell. But as soon as we went our different ways, I got through catering college with flying colours and Jim turned out to be really clever.'

As children, they used to compete to see who could assemble the more impressive collection of tropical fish and it was just as Jamie seemed to be inching ahead that his thermostat broke and he woke up in the morning to the tank full of simmering fish. Jim reckoned that was when Jamie took an interest in cooking.

When Jim went off travelling round the world for a year, Jamie was desperately jealous that he was not going with him but he had just moved to

London to get his career going and he didn't have the cash to finance a year away. But he made sure Jim got a good send-off with a big leaving party at his dad's pub. Jamie spent all day making the pizzas and his band provided the music. When Jim was a student up in Coventry and Jamie's wealth arrived with a vengeance, both friends made sure the money did not come between them.

'Jamie is an absolute diamond,' said 'Simon', a pal who prefers to keep his identity a secret. 'We were friends at school and then we lost touch for quite a while. I knew he was a cook and I saw him in London once or twice, just for a drink. I had a good job in marketing and I was doing really well at first. I had a smart flat in Docklands and a convertible BMW and I thought life was sweet. But some of the guys at work introduced me to the drugs scene. We used to go out all weekend and get totally blasted. We didn't feel like we were doing any harm but gradually we began supplying drugs. At first, it was just a few tablets of E and some blow. There are loads of straight guys who like to freak out and don't exactly move in the sort of circles where you can get drugs. I was just bridging the gap, or so I thought. But it was so lucrative I got really greedy.

'Pretty soon I was making more money from

drug-dealing than I was out of my job. But a group of us made a major cock-up at work due to being completely spaced out and it cost the company quite a lot of money. My so-called friends were quick to pass all the blame my way and I was out of a job when my bosses found out what I had been up to. I was lucky not to go to prison. And I was homeless because I got evicted from my flat for not paying the rent.

'My family had all broken up after I left home. My dad gave my mum a pretty hard time and they split up and they both had new lives without much space in them for an out-of-work son with a drug habit and no prospects.

'It was just when Jamie was making it really big, so he was the last person I expected to hear from. But an old girlfriend had told him what a mess I'd made of my life. He was brilliant. He didn't lecture me but he did bollock me and tell me in no uncertain terms what a monumental mess I was making of my life. He didn't give me money directly but he got me a job and helped me to find somewhere to live. He promised to help me so long as I worked hard at it and stayed off drugs. He made damn sure I kept my side of the bargain and he helped me out with a deposit when I wanted a flat. It's all behind me now. I've got a career and a new girlfriend and a new life but I could have gone right down. Jamie never forgets his friends and his background. He might be a great chef on TV but he is even better as a mate.'

'Jamie has always been the same,' says Peter Begg, a fellow chef from The River Café days. 'You should see him in the kitchen at work. It is fantastic what he is doing. I have long believed what he believes that you don't really need recipes, just an understanding of what you are supposed to be doing when you are cooking. Jamie? Changed? It would take an awful lot more than a TV series to change Jamie. He is an ordinary bloke – well, actually, he's not. He is pretty amazing and he is a very good cook. There are not many Jamies around.'

'Jamie has not changed,' says musician Daniel Jones, a friend from catering college and who worked in The Cricketers. 'Where we're from, it's weird – we all go off and do different things, but no one has ever really changed.'

Contrary to what some carping columnists have said recently, Jamie Oliver does not believe he has changed the world. But he is proud of what he has achieved in such a short time. 'In the last couple of years, we've tried to show that it's quite cool to cook,' says Jamie. 'You eat three times a day so you might as well eat well. Definitely, women do appreciate it. But anyone appreciates it, male or female. If you come home to a nice bit of tucker, it's kinda quite cool and romantic. It's quite a good pulling factor. I've been with the same bird for nine years but girls do seem to go for it. I've made so many converts but I still have a percentage of people who want to chase me down the road and beat pulp out of me. It's a life of two sides.'

But it makes for a busy life. 'I've been cutting my own hair for three months now because I haven't had time to go to the bloomin' hairdresser.'

Jamie's openness is natural, not an act, and sometimes he knows he goes too far. Jools was embarrassed when Jamie answered a cheeky journalist's question, 'When did you last feel utterly insignificant?' with the headline-hitting response, 'Last night when I was in bed with my missus and I lasted three seconds.'

Jamie loves clothes and that studied scruffiness takes a great deal of achieving. 'My latest pride and joy is a top Duffer jacket. The more I wear it and the more I get it dirty and scratched, the better it's going to look.'

Jamie admits his taste in clothing is quite stuck in the '70s. 'I've got about five sets of Gazelles and Campus and I like the old denim. I often shop in second-hand stores, so it's not so much about an item of clothing as a certain period.'

Jamie's love for Jools is total and all-consuming. He says that he thinks the three essential ingredients of love are trust, respect ... and lust. If he were allowed to write just one last letter to someone, it would be to Jools and it would say simply: 'I love you, make sure you thank everyone for everything.' He will always be grateful to her for the massive support she has given him. She hates flying but she has put her fears to one side to travel with him on his endless globe-trotting trips. And Jamie's remedy for those interminable flights is another example of his cheeky take on life. He reckons the worst aspect of air travel is that airlines don't help passengers join the mile-high club. 'They'd only need a little room, a couple of handles to brace yourself. A little bit of a laugh for about three minutes ... if you do it twice.'

As the success grows and grows, Jamie is careful to make sure he always takes enough time off from his increasingly busy schedule to be with Jools. He says, 'We have little mini-holidays, just days off relaxing, really, but we rarely leave London. I've got a 50cc Velocifero, a very sexy retro-style Italian scooter, like a hairdryer on wheels, which is great for whacking down the park and parking cheekily up on the pavement. But the best breaks are on hot days in my garden at home. I get a stack of cold French beers in the freezer, Juliette sits in the sun and I tinker about planting things. I grow tomatoes, zucchini, French beans and loads of herbs – thyme, bay, rosemary, sage, oregano, marjoram – the lot. It's not that I am particularly green-fingered, I am just mad about food. If I ever have any influence, the first thing I will do is to whinge about herbs in the supermarkets. They really take the mick with the prices.

'The thing is, there is always a million things to do and I like to get them done. I can never just lie in the sun. But when I get away, my ideal holiday will be anywhere hot, for more than two days with nothing to do but read, drink beer and spend quality time with Juliette, a proper chill-out time. Then I will happily sit there all day and do nothing.'

After spending all their adult lives together, Jamie and Jools are still blissfully happy. As Jamie puts it, 'The Olivers are like swans. Once we find a mate, it's for life. Jools is a good girl. When we first met she was too nice, almost to the point of being a drip. But these past two years she has just got so strong. If anybody criticises me, it upsets her, because I am part of her now.'

Jamie's relationship with Jools is based on total trust. Lots of female admirers have found out first hand that he is not interested in other women. And one or two well-known ladies have made it clear they would like more than just another helping. But Jamie has his own rules. He believes that even a full-on kiss means you are being unfaithful. 'As soon as you kiss them, then you've gone past the line. But men are weak. Anything beyond a cuddle is too far.'

Old friend Gennaro says, 'Jools is a lovely girl. Of course, she is going to worry a lot, he is a superstar. But with Jamie there is no trouble.'

Jamie says, 'I know how her mind works and she knows how mine works. I do short-change her in time a lot now, but she trusts me. She knows I am not going off gallivanting, screwing other girls. I have never been unfaithful and I can look her in the eye and say that. It is just a really nice feeling.'

And in any case, Jamie admits there is one thing at which he is absolutely hopeless – lying. 'I'm a shit liar. I flinch, I go red, my eyes go funny.' Jamie has no experience of ditching girlfriends and he hopes that he never has to learn. But when asked, he advised not too wisely, 'Give them a kiss, tell them that you love them.'

Now well into his twenties Jamie is convinced that he is in the process of turning into his father. He said, 'I filmed a programme with him, and when it got down to editing it, all our body movements were exactly the same. I think I have the same querying look.'

Chapter Fourteen

Starting a Family

Like most super successful people in Britain, Jamie Oliver finds that there is an inevitable backlash to his rise and rise. In the summer of 2001, as Jamie put the final touches to his third BBC series and prepared for his ambitious Happy Days tour of cookery on stage for the autumn, he found himself under fire. Jamie gave one of his usual, frank and enthusiastic interviews to the *Daily Telegraph*, but the headline I DON'T WANT PEOPLE TO THINK I'M A PRAT suggested the challenging tone of the piece. Jamie was accused of not being genuinely involved in the cooking at Montes, of being 'whipped into a froth of cheffy superstardom', even of being 'irritating' as he slid down his famous spiral staircase. Jamie rose to the bait and said, 'If someone thinks I'm a prat and annoying, I kinda wanna know why, really. 'Cos I don't want to be a prat. But if people don't like me just for being me, then fair enough … at the end of the day, they can always switch over or not buy the book. I'm 26 and I've made a lot of money and you know what? It pisses a lot of people off.'

This level of honesty is unusual in ordinary people. In an A-list celebrity it is almost unheard of. But it didn't stop the *Telegraph* carping at everything from his accent to his deal with Sainsbury's. And who could fail to respond when Jamie boldly suggested that he was the 'ambassador of British cooking across the world'? He said, 'I have done more for English food throughout the world in the past two years than anyone else has done in the past 100 years. I have put it on the map.'

Jamie explained his international success and said forcefully that, when he went on American chat shows, he stood up for British cooking, but it was not easy. 'They think the British are a load of heathens who eat greasy old toad in the hole with mad cows and BSE and salmonella. They think we eat slop.'

It was colourful, outspoken stuff and the usual suspects lined up to sneer afterwards that Jamie Oliver was clearly getting much too big for his trendy trainers. They forgot one small point, of course. Everything Jamie said was true. He does stand up and be counted on all the important food issues. He is passionate about what he does. And he knows perfectly well that there will be people who don't like him. Every major television figure from Bob Monkhouse to David Frost knows that if you have a style that is strongly individual you are going to polarise opinion.

Jamie is perfectly happy if people who don't like him don't watch. He just wants to be able to entertain and inspire the vast majority of millions who do get turned on to cookery by the guy from Essex.

He doesn't get too upset by the critics. He knows he has seriously pushed cooking on to another level in Britain.

It is part of the essential Jamie Oliver appeal that he does not compromise his principles. He is being himself on television and he is enthusiastic about cookery. He loves food and entertaining people, and the work ethic ingrained in him from an early age back at The Cricketers by his parents drives him on and on.

Jamie had his third series of *The Naked Chef* on BBC television in the autumn of 2001, and his programmes have been seen in 64 countries around the world. He loves people coming up and telling him they saw him baking bread in Peru, but he refuses to worry about over-exposure. Although the Sainsbury's adverts have certainly raised the Oliver profile, Jamie does not appear on chat shows and you certainly will not see him appearing on game shows like *Ready, Steady Cook!*

The one new development which brought smiles all round in the Oliver household was the news of the baby, and in September 2001 came the happy news that Jools was pregnant.

Jamie was delighted, and astonished that the news seemed to have leaked out so quickly. But it perhaps explained why he was seen wearing a permanent ear-to-ear smile as the summer drew to a close. Friends knew that Jools and Jamie had been trying desperately hard to start a family. The couple were upset to learn some months previously that Jools suffered from a condition which could affect her fertility, but were greatly heartened to learn that it was treatable. The baby was expected to be born at the end of March and Jamie was already planning to take a huge chunk out of his relentless schedule so he can give Jools and the baby the attention he knows they deserve. 'They have to come first from now on,' said Jamie. 'Now Jools has got a bun in the oven she has told me, "Right, you little so-and-so, it's time to sort yourself out." For the last three years I've been working seven days a week and Jools has been so patient in that time. We've been together for nine years and after eighteen months, when we started to get serious and talk about moving in together, I sat her down and explained a few things about the life of a chef. I told her the hours were very anti-social, involved working weekends and bank holidays and the like and she said, "Yeah, yeah, yeah." She has been great to put up with all that and more but now she is demanding I take weekends off and she also wants me to take more holidays. She wants me to take time off when the baby comes and I am not even arguing. The truth is I don't have a choice. Jools has put her foot down. I am looking forward to being with just the three of us. I can hardly wait.'

Jamie took a dramatic step back from his workaholic lifestyle so that he could enjoy the experience of becoming a father to the maximum. Even after trying so hard the pregnancy took them both by surprise. Jamie said, 'Neither of us was expecting it. We had been trying for ages and the old saying about trying so hard for something that it doesn't happen is so very true. The human body is very clever. It's got to be comfortable with what is going on and as soon as we chilled out about the situation, it happened and that was absolutely marvellous. I am still a little nervous about it all and I have got a lot of reading up to do over the next few months. To be honest, if you put a baby and a nappy in front of me at the moment, the poor kid would probably end up with it on his head.' But by the time his most important production arrived, The Naked Chef promised to be a properly prepared and pukka parent.

Jamie felt as though he had been waiting for years to be a dad, but when the great moment came it almost took him by surprise. Jools started getting contractions just as the couple were finally moving into their new house. She was already four days late and the couple were so caught up in the problems of moving they almost forgot about the impending arrival. But baby Poppy Honey certainly made herself felt. Jamie was shocked as he saw his beautiful wife go through 30 hours of labour before finally giving birth. Jamie was stunned. His love for his wife was suddenly combined with awe and admiration of what she had achieved. Jamie was well aware of the cliché but he insisted several hundred times afterwards that this really was the proudest moment of his life. Poppy Honey Oliver weighed in at 7lb 14oz when she was born, at 3.20pm on March 19, 2002 at Queen Charlotte's and Chelsea Hospital.

It took a while for parenthood to sink in but both Jamie and Jools were overwhelmed with emotion at the experience. Jamie told a close friend that although he had tried to prepare himself for the experience, so that he could be as helpful as possible to Jools, the sheer wonder of the birth simply blew him away. 'Now I know why people are never quite the same after they have had kids,' said Jamie. 'All of a sudden there is this little tiny person who you love more than you thought possible. She is so wonderful and so totally dependent on us that it is awesome.'

Jamie was determined to be a very hands-on father but he admits he was not exactly enthusiastic about some of the messier tasks. Changing Poppy's nappies wasn't his favourite job. 'I hate bodily functions,' says Jamie. 'I try to approach it like a mechanic. You know, if something is wrong, work from one end to the other. Is she hot, cold, hungry, thirsty? Does she want winding, changing?'

The arrival of Poppy Honey was a welcome diversion from the contract wrangling with the BBC that occupied the earlier part of 2002. After three highly successful series, and more than £1.3million in book sales, Jamie was keen to maintain his relationship with the Corporation. But the BBC was increasingly uneasy about Jamie's link with supermarket chain Sainsbury's in a string of popular commercials. With a brand of Jamie Oliver products on sale within the store and the public backing of Sainsbury's chief executive Sir Peter Davis, this was a link Jamie Oliver was unwilling to break. Jamie also wanted more control of his future and had set his heart on a new series, to be called Oliver's Army, which featured him running a non-profit-making restaurant in east London where he wanted to train and nurture underprivileged youngsters to become chefs, an idea that was to surface later with his controversial series, *Jamie's Kitchen*. *The Naked Chef* was a huge hit for the BBC with high ratings and sales to more than 30 countries. But the BBC was uncomfortable with the potential conflict of interest caused by the commercial links established by their charismatic star and pulled out of talks for a new series.

The BBC said: 'Having discovered Jamie and developed his career, we wish him the very best with his future ventures.' Jamie responded: 'I have loved working with the BBC over the past three years and I'm disappointed I will not be working with them on a new series.' Jamie was soon in demand from rival broadcasters and it wasn't long before he found a new home with Channel 4.

Chapter Fifteen

Jamie Confidential

Millionaire Jamie Oliver could have chosen the easy option and cashed in on his astonishing Naked Chef success on the BBC. He could have churned out more chirpy cookery programmes for commercial channels, backed up by the inevitable booming book sales. But instead he had an idea. He wanted to set up a brand new restaurant, staffed by untrained, unemployed youngsters who desperately needed a break after a difficult start in life. And he wanted all the profits to go to a charity to help other young people to pursue cookery careers.

Advisers and TV producers alike shook their heads in disbelief at the expense and impracticality of the plan, but Jamie was not to be diverted. He knew from first hand experience what it was like to be hard up and in need of help and he was determined to push ahead with his dream. He had been nurturing the scheme in his head for some eight years after a friend, who worked as a counsellor for underprivileged children, had remarked how cookery seemed to focus some of her most difficult charges. Kids who had been out of control one minute could become quite focussed and even sensitive the next when they became involved in preparing a meal. It was an image close to Jamie's heart and now he had the chance to do something about it.

Jamie's painful memories of his own difficult schooldays flooded back when he had to fight hard to put this difficult, edgy idea into practice. But the young man who has dealt with dyslexia and the 'special needs' jeers of his schoolmates has developed remarkable willpower and sense of purpose. Even so, the reality of finding somewhere to start the business, of dealing with young people who were largely strangers to the concept of hard work, and making the whole thing work as a viable business was much, much harder than he could ever have imagined. Suitable premises were eventually found in Shoreditch, East London and fifteen young people were recruited. All of them were in need of a helping hand in life, but not all of them knew how to take it.

It was a business, a TV programme and an enormous challenge. The history of establishing new restaurants is littered with expensive disasters. But at every hint of crisis Jamie's response was to work harder. He simply refused to accept even the prospect of defeat.

The sight of an increasingly anguished Jamie struggling to persuade, cajole and even bully his inexperienced workforce into shape was inspirational. As *Jamie's Kitchen* hit Channel 4 screens in Britain and countless other channels around the world, before their very eyes viewers could see a young man, who had earned the sort of wealth most people can only dream about, putting something back into society. The problems were enormous and sometimes seemed insuperable. Some days the workers simply did not arrive and Jamie's frustration turned into a four-letter fury. Some of the confrontations were angry and tearful and they made for electrifying television.

Jools soon found her husband had become taken over by his dedication to Fifteen, the name of the groundbreaking restaurant, and she was unhappy when some of their disagreements on the subject became included in the programme. Only eight of the original fifteen young workers stayed the course and became qualified chefs. During their training they cooked for the Prince of Wales, Tony Blair and Irish Prime Minister Bertie Ahern. Jamie's passionate enthusiasm for the project and the reactions of his young workers made the documentary series a hit in Britain and around the world. 'Filming this programme has made me realise human beings are not robots,' said Jamie. 'And it made me understand the importance of family and family structure. At Fifteen we became a second family. It was a real project. We had real goals.'

But even though he was not going to personally profit from the restaurant, Jamie knew Fifteen had to succeed as a business as well as a reality TV series. He had poured much of the money he earned from the Sainsbury's adverts to finance the restaurant and the whole enterprise went horrendously over budget from the start. When cash ran dangerously short he risked his own home to back the project. Jools was pregnant at the time so Jamie kept most of the more alarming details of the arrangement from her. When some of the workers questioned Jamie's motives he shocked them with some financial straight-talking about the depth of his own investment that worked wonders.

And if the pressure on the star sometimes meant that his language was a shade colourful for some viewers, well that was understandable. As Jamie said, 'People have asked, "Why did you swear so much on the show?" and I say, "Have you ever put your house down on something you're never going to make a penny out of?"'

Inspite of the inevitable last minute hitches the restaurant was launched to rave reviews and has been virtually fully booked every since. 'We get 5,000 phone calls every day,' says Jamie. 'And when you've only got 65 seats that means a lot of disappointed people. It's crazy, every day is always go, go, go.'

The pioneering enterprise brought Jamie the honour of an MBE for his 'services to the hospitality industry' and he managed to hit the headlines when he arrived at Buckingham Palace to collect his award without a tie. He was dressed in a smart Paul Smith suit but he said afterwards, 'I like ties, but I prefer not to wear one when I'm nervous. They said wear whatever you're comfortable in. At 28, I think I'm the youngest person receiving an award today.'

Happily by autumn 2003 the restaurant was making its first profits. They all go to Jamie's Cheeky Chops charity which helps to teach the young unemployed how to cook, with training supplemented by work experience at top London restaurants like The Ivy and The River Café.

Every six months a new crop of 15 recruits is taken on by Jamie Oliver. They do their basic training at Hammersmith and West London College before joining Fifteen. 'I am committed to the project for life, financially and mentally,' says Jamie.

At home Jamie Oliver's other commitments grew even more dramatically. Daisy Boo was born on April 10, 2003 just a year and three weeks after the birth of Jools and Jamie's first child, Poppy Honey. And second time around it was a much easier experience for all concerned. Jools was taking fertility drugs to help her conceive and she was desperately worried that she might never be able to have children. 'All I could do was be there for her,' said Jamie afterwards. He was delighted when she fell pregnant naturally the second time. 'It was a miracle,' said Jamie. 'I'm over the moon. Jools was brilliant during the birth and we're just really proud of the new addition to the family.'

Daisy weighed in at 8lb 4oz and arrived nine days overdue after a two hour labour at Queen Charlotte's and Chelsea Hospital in White City, west London. Daisy has the name of a flower like her sister Poppy and Boo is also one of her mother's nicknames. As the couple left hospital with their second daughter Jamie joked, 'See you again next year,' with the staff.

Jools said, 'I was actually pregnant twice within the same year so I've been sick most mornings now for what seems like forever. However I do love having a fat tummy.'

Family is clearly the main priority for Jamie now and he and Jools both imagine eventually having more children. 'But not yet,' says Jamie. 'Two is enough for a while. I don't want to miss any of their growing up.'

When Poppy Honey was one, Jamie and Jools celebrated with plenty of presents but they also bought her a tree. 'I thought I'd buy her a cherry tree, plant it, and in 10 years time she'll have something to remember about her first birthday.'

Jamie's Kitchen was a huge hit in the United States where he was featured on five consecutive editions of the top-rated *Today* show. Millions watched as Jamie tested to see if his meringue was firm by holding the bowl over his head and covered himself. Guest Dustin Hoffman was impressed and suggested he would like to turn Jamie's story into a film. The rags to riches aspect of *Jamie's Kitchen* has also attracted other movie interest but the young chef is wary of talking about the plans in detail.

But when Brad Pitt asked Jamie to fly to Los Angeles to cook a special meal for him and wife Jennifer Aniston in February 2004 he had to agree, and Jamie and Jools had a great time with their film star friends.

Chapter Sixteen

Turkey Twizzlers and Number 10 Calling

The success of Fifteen was remarkable, and it was sustained as the restaurant in Hoxton, in east London, was followed by similar establishments in Amsterdam and Melbourne as well as another in Britain in Cornwall's Watergate Bay in 2006.

Jamie is rightly proud of Fifteen and highly supportive of all the apprentice chefs who reach his high standards. He is a demanding leader but he is also very thoughtful and considerate to his young charges. Some students were missing classes because they were smoking cannabis. That would have seen them sacked by some establishments but Jamie did not throw them out. He brought in drug counsellors to help them to kick their habit and regain control of their lives.

After Fifteen came *Jamie's School Dinners*, the BAFTA-winning Channel Four series which also took two National Television Awards and put Turkey Twizzlers into the headlines and took them off the plates of pupils across the land.

Helped by the unforgettable Nora Sands, the inspirational dinner lady from Greenwich, Jamie took on the problem of the declining standards in school meals. The trouble started with the cutting of domestic science from the curriculum and the privatising of school catering services in 1989. Jamie's campaign to improve school meals quickly caught the public's imagination. In *Jamie's School Dinners*, he toured school canteens and revealed how desperately bad the food was that was prepared for children. In response, the then Secretary of State for Education, Ruth Kelly, announced in September 2005 that foods which were high in fat, sugar and salt were to be banned from school meals and vending machines.

The decline in the quality of school meals was quick and undeniable. With his new-found fame Jamie was constantly being quizzed about the problem and he was concerned. He agreed that they were dreadful but then realised that he was in a position to do something about it.

It all started when Jamie went to visit the outspoken dinner lady Nora Sands at Kidbrooke School in Greenwich, south London, to take a look at what the children of today had for lunch. He was stunned by the poor quality of what was on offer. He homed in on the dreaded Turkey Twizzler, with its alarmingly low meat and high fat content, for a headline-hitting onslaught. 'Turkey Twizzlers are a symbol of everything I hate in school dinners,' said Jamie. 'They should be banned. They are insulting to kids.'

Jamie was very passionate about children's right to have decent food. And he was not shy about telling it like it was. He was outraged to see a young mother giving her one-year-old an unsuitable drink and said to the *Sunday Times*: 'If you're giving your young children fizzy drinks, you're an arsehole, you're a tosser. If you give them bags of crisps you're an idiot.'

Jamie's genuine anger was what turned a television series into a life-changing experience for millions of schoolchildren. He was simply outraged to find that many pupils come to school without eating any breakfast, then have the same sort of sandwich for lunch every day of the week and often go without a cooked meal at home in the evening. It was wrong, and he knew instinctively that he was unearthing a national scandal. As with everything he gets involved with, Jamie took it personally. At several points in *Jamie's School Dinners* he was so emotional that he looked close to tears as he raged about the deplorable standard of school meals. 'It's frustrating,' he said. 'It makes me feel bad about cooking and it makes me hate food.'

He was shown in the canteen of Eden Community School in Peterlee, County Durham, toying with a piece of fish product called Monster Feet and grumbling, 'I can see a bit of onion and bread, but I honestly have no idea what this is. We are sitting here in a beautiful room surrounded by beautiful children. It's the most important time in their life and they're being fed this... These kids deserve better.' Monster Feet joined Turkey Twizzlers on Jamie's hit-list of school meal horrors. He was incensed that the products had been minced up, added to, formed into an interesting shape, which was then coated with breadcrumbs or batter to make it appealing to kids. 'Generally they are high in fat and salt, and if you look at the list of ingredients they will often show a meat or fish content of only forty per cent or less,' said Jamie. 'You may also notice the addition of extra skin or pork fat.'

The scale of the problem often surprised Jamie as much as the viewers. He was astonished when a paediatrician told him, 'If the things I see on the inside of children were on the outside then it would be classed as child abuse.' The doctor revealed to Jamie some x-rays of a child whose intestines were so badly blocked that he had not been able to go to the toilet in weeks. The doctor said, 'If you change his diet I won't have to see him any more.'

Jamie wanted more than just decent school dinners. He wanted home economics back in the curriculum. As he put it, 'When kids leave school at sixteen they should be able to survive. They should know how to buy food economically, how to freeze things, and how to cook a roast and a curry and a stir fry. You can learn all you like about chemistry or physics but at the end of the day you have to eat.'

Jamie's knack for asking the awkward question at times elevated the series into electrifying television. He asked the squirming Education Secretary Alan Johnson, 'Why can't we ban junk food altogether?' Johnson looked as if he was wondering why he had agreed to face the cameras and suggested it might infringe civil liberties. 'We ban drugs,' said Jamie simply. He went on: 'There does need to be somebody saying, "F*** me, kids are getting bigger and they are getting fatter and they're dropping dead younger." This is the first generation of kids that is going to die before their parents. Someone has to get strong, someone has to be the governor and you don't have to like them!'

The directness of Jamie's message was irresistible. 'After the programme went out there was so much anger from parents,' said Jamie. 'It was the talk of the school gates. Parents were not happy and teachers were not happy.'

Jamie's delivery of a petition to Downing Street with 271,677 signatures was quickly followed by new rules based on recommendations by the School Meals Review Panel and the School Food Trust. Strict nutritional standards were brought in which banned the sale of fizzy drinks, crisps and chocolate on school premises and restricted deep-fried food like chips to twice a week. Hot dogs, burgers and the infamous Turkey Twizzlers were to be replaced by high quality meats, oily fish and two daily portions of fruit and vegetables.

In the end, Jamie got to see Tony Blair face to face at Number 10 and with a General Election looming the Prime Minister agreed to all the demands. There was to be an extra £240 million to help pay for the new healthy eating regime in schools up to 2011 and £2 million to help establish training kitchens for staff.

'I did get the impression that the government were ambushed,' admitted Jamie with characteristic honesty. 'But it is their job to listen. And they couldn't deny the powerful response from the parents.' Jamie could not care less that the Prime Minister might have seen backing the campaign as a vote winner. He had invested eighteen months of considerable effort and energy, working alongside dinner ladies and bringing the scandal of school meals into the public eye. 'All I wanted was more money on the plate, dinner ladies trained better, school kitchens repaired and nutritional standards raised to a decent level,' he said.

'Making four powerful programmes is great but actually changing things for millions of kids in brilliant.' And Jamie's close friend, the film star Brad Pitt, for whom Jamie cooked on his fortieth birthday, could not have agreed more. 'Brad thinks the project is brilliant,' Jamie told the *News of the World*. 'In fact he wants me to do it in America because where he comes from is one of the most unhealthy parts of the US. Brad wouldn't eat Turkey Twizzlers or any of that s**t, but when he is next over I'll get my favourite dinner lady Nora to cook him a school meal.'

Jamie Oliver never rests on his laurels and he was keen to change course quickly. Jamie's idea to travel to Italy for a new television series was born out of a desire to get back to his first love of cooking. He was understandably irritated when, after the recent worthy screen work, this was written off by some critics as a quick money-spinner. It was a daft suggestion in any case, as cash had long since ceased to be a motivation for Jamie. This was the original Jamie Oliver revelling in the joys of preparing food as a welcome alternative from trying to change the world. He said at the time, 'Fifteen was about the basics of cooking, training cooks and helping out some people who needed helping. *School Dinners* was about doing miracles with 37p and improving the diet of our young people. It was never going to provide the most orgasmic food but it was a job that desperately needed doing.'

For three or four years, it had all been about other people rather than himself, Jamie reflected. But now he wanted to unleash his old enthusiasm for food on a country he loved – Italy. 'I've always loved Italy and wanted to get away from it all driving around and cooking,' Jamie told the *Sunday Times*. 'There is such diversity in lifestyles, cooking traditions and dialects. That is why as a chef I find Italy so damn exciting. I should have been Italian.'

The concept behind the show was to spend six weeks motoring in a battered old camper van from Sicily to Le Marche, cooking for all sorts of different people, from fishermen and farmers to a countess and a road-sweeper, as it turned out. Jamie's beloved van had earlier been restored to rather more than its former glory, as the vehicle-loving chef had installed a Porsche engine to improve performance vastly. But, for the series, it had to tow a heavy trailer carrying a makeshift kitchen and not surprisingly it broke down several times. 'To be honest it was a complete pain in the arse,' said Jamie frankly. But the van was soon repaired and the tour was completed.

It was really important to Jamie to set off into the sunset. 'I never had a boys' holiday, never went away travelling, and I just thought after the last four years I wanted to submerge myself into hardcore cooking. For the last year and a half I've been submerged in Turkey Bleedin' Twizzlers and I wanted to do something else. I love Italy, everything about it. I'd love to get a farmhouse on the Amalfi coast.'

High ratings quickly followed, especially after Jamie controversially slaughtered a lamb in one programme.

The television ideas certainly keep coming. In 2007, *Jamie's Chef* saw trainees from Fifteen competing to win a pub put up by the charity. Fifteen now makes a profit and Jamie is determined to use that money to help his chefs get on their feet with businesses of their own. The contest to win The Cock in Beazley End, near Braintree in Essex, was tense and entertaining, and Jamie said afterwards, 'I am really proud of what all my graduates have achieved.'

But the price of success is often high. Jamie grumbles: 'I'm a brand. That's what people see me as. But I'm also a person so I am vulnerable.' Experience has taught him to ration his time much more carefully. He now insists that weekends are precious family times to be spent with Jools and their two daughters and he always builds in a long summer break into his relentless schedule.

Life in the public spotlight is never easy, and sensitive Jools has wisely reined in the amount of exposure of her young family she was prepared to allow the television cameras. Jamie did permit transmission of a scene where Jools was upset over tabloid claims that the marriage was in crisis. He explained that while he regretted the level of fame he had acquired, he recognised that it was a key part of everything he has achieved. He told the *Sunday Times*, 'It was an emotional scene and Jools was crying. But I thought "F*** it, they've got to see the effect of what they write."' The so-called marriage troubles were a tabloid invention. 'Jools and I love each other to bits,' said Jamie.

And now he is wise enough now to put family time at the very top of his priorities. 'My idea of a perfect day is when the kids are asleep, the fire's lit and I'm having a siesta in the afternoon on the sofa with my missus,' says Jamie. 'And I love to spend time cooking with my daughters. They love to cook anything, as long as they can get involved and touch it. Cake is always good because they can eat it as they're going along.'

Jamie enjoys life and all his many successes, and he was especially knocked out by his achievement in changing government policy. Many pundits suggested he would be in line for a knighthood to follow his MBE. Typically, Jamie was not too impressed: 'It would be a nice compliment to get a knighthood but I don't think my mates would have it. They'd refuse to call me Sir Jamie – it would be more likely Sir T**ser!'

Chapter Seventeen

Onwards and
Upwards

In autumn 2007 Jamie showed he had no
intention of slowing down his whirl-
wind work schedule as he announced that he
intended to establish a chain of Italian
restaurants, perhaps not surprisingly called
'Jamie's Italian'. Always an enthusiast of Italian
cuisine, he was delighted when the first branch
opened in Oxford, the following May. From the
start, it proved very successful and others soon
followed in Bath, Kingston, Brighton, Cardiff,
Guildford, Cambridge, Reading, Glasgow, Leeds,
Liverpool, Birmingham, Nottingham and Bristol.
There were also three branches in London

(Covent Garden, Canary Wharf and Islington) and another in Dubai.

Jamie's high hopes for the project were quickly fulfilled, which was remarkable in a period when many other restaurants foundered, including the flagships of other television chefs like Antony Worrall Thompson. There was a simple reason for this success, which as he explained, was down to giving great value for money. He said: 'We're fortunate because we don't overstretch ourselves financially, plus we're doing fantastic food at great prices at Jamie's Italian. Essentially we're doing a £40 meal for £20 and with brilliant service. How can we do that? By getting a lot of people through the door. And so far pretty much everyone who has visited Jamie's Italian has wanted to come back, again and again.'

The flow of new ideas and innovative television programmes from the energetic chef hit a new high in 2008 as Jamie fronted the thought-provoking *Eat To Save Your Life* (Channel 4), using detailed research and shock tactics to try and improve the eating habits of millions of badly nourished viewers. The show included a horrifying autopsy by Dr Gunther von Hagens on the body of a man who had ballooned to 159 kilos (25 stone), thanks to his disastrous diet. The same year, *Jamie's*

Fowl Dinners focused on some of the more alarming aspects of the British poultry business and made it clear that unless the public were prepared to pay more for their poultry products then the whole industry could be in serious trouble. Remarkably, the response from both the RSPCA and the farming industry was extremely positive, and a speedy rise in sales of free range and organic products was reported.

It was all interesting stuff but Jamie's next TV project hit even more headlines. He chose the 'typically British' town of Rotherham, with a population of a quarter of a million in the heart of South Yorkshire, to launch the controversial *Ministry of Food* (Channel 4). It is anything but a prosperous area and the only way the region was booming was around the waistline as Rotherham was allegedly heading towards becoming the fattest town in the land. Jamie's aim was to transform the whole country to become healthier, live longer and enjoy a better relationship with food; according to him, the real work began in the homes of Rotherham families. At the outset, he said: 'I have no idea what's going to happen in the next six months. All I can say is if *School Dinners* was like *Star Wars*, then *Ministry of Food* is going to be like *The Empire Strikes Back!*'

With characteristic confidence, he began his quest by confronting the only person he knew of in Rotherham: Julie Critchlow, the lady who had attempted to undermine his campaign for healthier school dinners by passing chips and junk food to schoolchildren through the playground fence. 'In my view she represents everything that's wrong with our relationship with food in this country,' said Jamie. 'Those pictures of Julie putting the burgers through the railings have been seen in all 56 countries that I work in.'

The meeting was great television as it was edged with anticipation after Jamie described the ladies pushing fast food to the kids as 'big old scrubbers' on TV. He had the good grace to apologise and did his best to win the Critchlow family over to the healthy food cause. As it turned out, Mrs Critchlow did agree with much of what he had been saying about the importance of healthy eating and proved an invaluable addition to the series.

Jamie then used his wonderfully natural common touch to even greater effect as he went out with a camera crew, knocking on the doors of lots of hard-pressed mums, who were relying a little too heavily on takeaways for family meals. He discovered some shocking situations, with households who completely ignored the cooker yet were crying out for help and education. Afterwards, he exploded with expletive-laced anger at the system, which has hard-up families wasting precious income on expensive and far from nourishing junk food.

As usual with Jamie Oliver, this was compelling television. The sight of a mum explaining that her young daughter had already lost teeth because of her dreadful diet was seriously upsetting. Jamie was visibly moved and typically blunt: 'It's 2008 – I've been to Soweto and I've seen kids in AIDS orphanages eating better stuff than that!' Yet somehow he managed to remain optimistic throughout: 'If we can get mates teaching mates, I think we can completely change the face of eating, shopping and health in England.' He was shocked to find women who had never boiled a pan of water and men who insisted chips were all they wanted: 'Everyone needs to take responsibility. It's about the home and it's about family. Everyone needs to listen.'

The people of Rotherham certainly listened to Jamie Oliver at his most persuasive, as did the rest of the country. In fact, the sight of those who had never considered eating food not covered in batter actually preparing their own, much healthier food for themselves and their children was inspirational Oliver at his best. A *Ministry of Food* headquarters was established by Jamie in the town centre to provide excellent back-up in the shape of information, cooking lessons and advice for locals keen to switch from endless takeaways to preparing more nutritious meals.

The service proved so popular that Rotherham Council took over and continued to run it; educational classes were heavily oversubscribed many months after the programme was screened. Not only that but a second *Ministry of Food* centre opened in Bradford in November 2009 and a third in Leeds (April 2010). In addition many other councils revealed they were actively pursuing the idea of providing similar assistance to try and solve the nation's ballooning obesity problem. At the same time, *Jamie's Ministry of Food* book became a huge national and international success, outstripping almost all of his other bestselling titles.

Jamie Oliver's ever-growing popularity in the United States led to an appearance on the top-rated *Oprah Winfrey Show* in 2010. Naturally, he was anxious to make a good impression but his arrival did not turn out quite as planned. He explained the mishap to Jeremy Clarkson in a highly entertaining guest appearance on BBC's *Top Gear*: 'We were in Chicago, and it was quite exciting because it's a huge and important show and very difficult to get on. They ran some video of lots of stuff I've done and it was a very proud moment in my life, with Oprah smiling at me as I went into this huge and beautifully-lit studio.' Somehow at the big moment in his rush to get on, Jamie tripped and: 'I went straight on the floor and skidded on my front for about four or five metres. And they had this awkward family of eaters from Chicago there to meet me. They were sitting round a table for four and I was going straight for them. It was just a really scary moment, but it was great. They left it in the show – I think they thought I was a stuntman!' He also revealed that he drives a Maserati. Clarkson was somewhat scornful of his choice, but Jamie insisted: 'I love it – it's beautiful!'

The highlight of the *Top Gear* appearance was Jamie attempting to prepare a salad in the back of his massively improved campervan while 'the Stig' drove it quickly round a racetrack. It was a very uncomfortable ride for Jamie, though a hilarious journey for the viewers – 'That was awful! I felt sick afterwards – he was really going for it and I couldn't see anything.' He also got the chance to try and beat rival celebrity chef Gordon Ramsay's time driving round the racetrack. 'Gordon Ramsay is a very good friend of mine and I've spent my whole life chasing him – now I want to beat him for once!'

he declared. As the viewers saw to their delight, he drove very well indeed and equalled the Ramsay time, then made sure his name was just above his rival's on the TV leader board.

The pace of Jamie Oliver's life rarely falters. Early in 2009, he took on the complex issue of pig husbandry and found himself sticking up for the hard-pressed British pig farmer in a Channel 4 documentary, *Jamie Saves Our Bacon*. Then, on 1 April, he made it a hat trick of appearances in charge of the kitchens of Number 10 Downing Street as he cooked for the presidents and prime ministers in London for the G20 talks. With a talented team, including an apprentice from Fifteen London, he put together a menu designed to show off British cooking at its best. And the very next day he was delighted to celebrate a much more personal occasion: the arrival of his third daughter, Petal Blossom Rainbow.

Later in the year he launched the enterprising direct selling business, Jamie at Home, and also set up a new high street cooking shop project called Recipease, a chain of food and kitchen shops where customers can get cooking lessons, in Battersea, with another branch opening soon afterwards in Brighton. Jamie then spent several months in the United States making a Channel 4 series with real export potential, *Jamie's American Road Trip*. It was an ambitious and eventually hugely enjoyable series, with Oliver determined to get a little further off the beaten track, unlike many previous TV documentary makers.

In Los Angeles he met Mexican former gang members, whose rehabilitation focused on food preparation. Then, in Wyoming, he travelled to the remotest area to spend time with cowboys living far from civilisation. He discovered food from Peru, Columbia, Egypt and spent time in Louisiana, hunting alligators.

Jamie certainly discovered a taste for America. His first major network series for US television, *Jamie Oliver's Food Revolution* opened on the ABC network in March 2010 and soon became a top-rated hit, winning a much-prized Emmy Award for Best Reality Series. The new series was boldly set in what was described as the nation's 'most obese town' and Jamie received a difficult reception. As he told the *Guardian*: 'The town didn't react very well to me being there and there was one fellow on the radio who did a lot of shit-stirring that caused six weeks of agro for me. No one really wanted to get involved or help – they thought we wanted to make them look stupid.' But he remained philosophical about the experience: 'It was brilliant!

Change is hard and if you're shining a light on one of the most unhealthy places in the world, it has to be a car crash – there's no pretty way.'

Not that Jamie was neglecting his home country. A new book and series called *Jamie Does* (Channel 4) saw the energetic star searching for new culinary ideas amid a string of short-haul flights from the UK to highlight unknown, yet authentic recipes and flavours far and wide in spring 2010. Later that year in September 2010, he ventured for the first time into Britain's world of daytime television with *30 Minute Meals*, a daily series aimed at showing how it was possible to cook a whole meal in half an hour. The idea certainly found favour with the fans as the book of the series, *Jamie's 30 Minute Meals*, became a spectacular bestseller.

Much more important, of course, was the birth of Jamie's fourth child and first son, Buddy Bear Maurice, on 15 September 2010. Jamie and Jools were delighted to have a boy to join their three daughters and Jamie admits that of all the many demands on his time and energy, his wife and children are the most important by far. He and Jools have a long established two-word saying that sums up their attitude: 'Family first' seems to say it all for the Olivers.

Jamie Oliver's passion for good cooking remains

gloriously undimmed after all these years and his determination to do all he can to improve food standards appears stronger than ever. Even as 2012 began, he was taking the cause to the very top and demanding to know from British Prime Minister David Cameron whether or not he remained committed to the continued investment in improving school food, particularly in the new academies.

Jamie did not quite receive a straight answer despite throwing down a feisty challenge to Cameron to improve the teaching of life skills, including cooking and food education, in, as he spelt out: 'The light of rocketing obesity rates in the UK and the spiralling costs to the National Health Service of diet related diseases.'

It is now getting on for 30 years since Jamie Oliver first found gainful employment in the food industry as an enthusiastic eight-year-old podding peas and peeling potatoes in the kitchen of his father's pub, The Cricketers in Clavering, Essex. Those three decades have seen his youthful interest in food develop into a driving passion that has made him into a cult figure, as well as a highly successful international brand.

Jamie's remarkable career has left him wiser and more experienced than the youthful Naked Chef we first saw, but he still refuses to compromise his principles when it comes to food. He launched into an angry attack on Education Minister Michael Gove in April 2012 for allowing flagship academy schools to lower meal standards for pupils. Close friends insist Jamie is largely unchanged by fame and fortune. He still insists that in spite of all the demands on his time his wife and children come 'first, second and third' in his personal list of priorities.